I CAN'T SEE WHAT YOU'RE SAYING

I CAN'T SEE WHAT YOU'RE SAYING

Elizabeth Browning

With a foreword by O. L. Zangwill,
Professor of Experimental Psychology,
University of Cambridge

COWARD, McCANN & GEOGHEGAN

NEW YORK

First American Edition 1973

Copyright © 1972 by Elizabeth Browning

SBN: 698-10520-6
Library of Congress Catalog Card Number: 73-75240

Printed in the United States of America

To J.K.

with lov

and I c   thanks for which there are no adequate
words t   lations and friends who listened to what
we were saying, tried to understand and consistently loved
Freddy

and specially to Gillian Freeman and Richard Simon whose
caring, encouragement and patience gave me the confidence to
write this book

Foreword

by O. L. Zangwill

Professor of Experimental Psychology
University of Cambridge

The problems which a physically or mentally handicapped child
may bring even to the best regulated families are too well known
to call for comment. But in the case of well-recognized forms
of infantile handicap such as cerebral palsy, epilepsy or severe
mental subnormality, at least the medical issues are clear and
social and educational management relatively well-organized.
Unfortunately, this is seldom so in the case of many less well-
recognized conditions, in which severe psychological handicap
may develop without such obvious signs of damage to the brain
as paralysis or convulsive seizures and without obvious defect of
general intelligence. Yet the social and educational disability in
such cases may be almost, if not quite, as crippling to the child
and distressing to its parents. Further, the situation is rendered
even more bewildering by the fact that diagnosis is often contro-
versial and appropriate educational facilities virtually non-
existent.

The author of this book describes with remarkable honesty and
totally without self-pity what it is like to be the mother of such
a child. Her son, born prematurely and of very low birth weight,
undoubtedly sustained a degree of brain damage at, or shortly
after, birth, which caused deafness for sounds of high frequency.
As a result, his ability to discriminate and learn to recognize a
number of important speech-sounds was appreciably reduced. In
addition, he almost certainly suffered from a condition known to
neurologists as developmental aphasia, which was unlikely to

have been wholly caused by his hearing disability. In this condition, speech develops late and imperfectly and there is often a failure of comprehension going well beyond the effects of partial deafness. Although the condition improves to some extent in course of time, it is apt to leave in its wake very serious difficulties in learning to read and to spell. These produce an educational backwardness out of all proportion to the child's intellectual level as assessed by conventional intelligence tests. In short, we have to do with selective learning disability due neither to lack of intelligence nor to lack of educational opportunity. It is a true educational handicap.

Elizabeth Browning relates clearly and factually the medical and educational history of her son—a story that reveals only too disconcertingly the inadequacy of our authorities when called upon to deal with problems of the kind which this intelligent and attractive little boy presented. Although almost everyone she consulted was sympathetic and well-meaning, her story illustrates only too well the frightening extent of ignorance and misunderstanding in regard to the specific language disorders of childhood. Her book will help many—doctors, psychologists and teachers as well as parents—to understand what a case of developmental aphasia is really like and how best to be of help.

Fortunately, children with a degree of disability as pronounced as that of Mrs Browning's son are relatively uncommon. But milder grades of developmental language disorder are far from rare. These are most commonly expressed in relatively late acquisition of speech and persistent backwardness in reading and spelling. This condition, which is now known as specific or developmental dyslexia, is far from unusual, particularly among boys, and is beginning to attract popular attention. Although its existence has been denied by some, the evidence is now so overwhelming that attempts to discredit it must be dismissed as obscurantist, if not downright mischievous. Parents and teachers of dyslexic children may take heart from Mrs Browning's story and come to see that even the most recalcitrant learning difficulties are not necessarily irremediable. True, the educational level attained by a dyslexic child remains as a rule well below that of a normal child of comparable intelligence, but with reasonable good fortune such a child may ultimately achieve a responsible position in modern society. Indeed the present writer has known at least one dyslexic who by exceptional diligence and cultivation of methods of study involving a minimum of reading, eventually achieved a University degree.

One may hope that this book will be widely read. Apart from its scientific and medical interest, it shows clearly what can be done by an intelligent, perceptive, and, above all, determined mother faced with a family problem totally outside the range of ordinary experience. Its author is a brave woman and her example will give heart to any parents who may have the ill-fortune to find themselves in a comparable predicament. Whether taken as a case history or simply as a very human story, this book will interest and impress everyone concerned with the understanding and conquest of educational disability.

O. L. Zangwill

The Psychological Laboratory,
Downing Street,
Cambridge.

I CAN'T SEE WHAT
YOU'RE SAYING

I

'. . . and the language is incredible, every other word begins with F and I don't mean fantastic.' I had to laugh. This was my son, the shoe-smith's apprentice, seventeen and a half years old, standing in our cobbled yard in the late summer sun, propping up his bicycle in his new TUF shoes, old jeans and darned jersey and his face smeared with grime from the forge, at the end of his first day's work and the beginning of his adult life.

As I gazed at him, taking in every detail of his face, as if I were seeing him for the first time, my mind flashed back over the years, as they say a man relives his life when drowning, to the five weeks spent in hospital when he was born. He arrived ten weeks premature, by Caesarian section and only the extreme care and devotion of nurses and doctors first saved us both and then kept him alive. I was trundled down the old Victorian corridors, Cheltenham-like in a wheel chair, when he was nine days old to peer through the glass panel of the special care nursery where the Sister in Charge tilted a small white box forward, raised the lid and put in her hand to remove a tiny pad, thus revealing the truth about my baby being my son. He was very, very small and very yellow, too fragile to touch, and I wondered could there ever be anything to cuddle.

After this brief moment of proof I was taken back to bed and some weeks later left the hospital on legs which wobbled so much I knew I would never run or jump again so long as I lived. My son was left behind for eight more weeks until he reached the grand weight of five-and-a-half pounds.

Then came the day to go and fetch him. The excitement in the household was intense and his two young sisters Jean and Heather were beside themselves with impatience. I returned to my hospital for which I had the deepest feelings of respect and gratitude, carrying a small suitcase filled with tiny garments. I was told to dress my baby and, gingerly at first, I set about the job. He seemed to slip through *all* the clothes, so in the end I settled for a vest and wrapped him up in a large Granny-made shawl.

When we reached home the girls rushed to welcome him. Their faces registered emotions of disbelief and disappointment and then changed to feelings of guilt as they quickly tried to put everything right by saying bright, brittle things like 'Nice baby'; but that evening when I prepared him for his bath and they saw the full glory of his round pink body with its tiny face and tendril-like arms and legs waving aimlessly, Heather said with much sympathy but total resignation, 'O Mummy, *Froggy*.'

Jean was five and a half and Heather four when Freddy was born and they were fascinated by this living doll that I had produced. They were both born in South Africa where we had gone after marrying at the end of the war. My husband had taken up a post teaching in a Diocesan school there and we had returned to England after six years and he was teaching in a public school at this time.

The days and weeks passed; Freddy grew fatter and fatter and I not only ran again but skipped and jumped and even played tennis. His sisters loved him dearly, they thrust their most precious toys into his tiny hands, they fought over who should push the pram, one of them would cry if he cried as if by her sharing his pain he could bear it better. Freddy lay in his pram looking neat and plump in his blue knitting and it seemed that all day and every day he smiled. Somebody gave me a string of plastic lambs which stretched across the front of his pram. He very soon reached up his arms and was able to snatch at them and make them spin round. I would put him out for a morning sleep after an indecently large bowl of porridge at ten, and his signal to the world that he had woken was never a cry but a frantic pinging of twirling plastic lambs. This beautiful, fat, placid, smiling child made no effort to sit up and had to be padded with cushions behind him at feeding time. At the late age of eighteen months he decided to take the trouble and sat well-balanced unaided. I did not worry, therefore, when at two he still did not walk. I would look at him and then at the stairs and sometimes at the end of the day wondered if I could manage his great weight under my arm, and often put off his bedtime moment hoping my husband would come home and carry him for me. Freddy had turned into a most loving and cuddly person.

By the time he was beginning to make some effort to walk, I decided it was time he spoke as well. He had been so undemanding all his life; his sisters acted like little handmaidens, large, regular meals were served him and he smiled. It seemed he had got everything so he never had the need to ask; but we wanted some more communication and I was longing to hear him say 'Mummy'.

One evening I was sitting on the edge of the bath drying him on my knee. We had a game of which he never tired when he was bounced and then dropped through my opened knees. When he fell he would laugh quite madly and sometimes we all became helpless, he enjoyed this nonsense so much. This indefatigable bundle of joy was lurching to and fro demanding more when I looked deeply into his eyes and said 'When are you going to say "Mummy"?'

Sharp darts seemed to pierce icily through my chest, and it was with a sickening sensation that I suddenly realized he had no idea at all what I was saying. I repeated the question and just got a happy smile. I knew he had registered nothing. My husband suggested I set traps for him to try to discover if he heard, so next day when the familiar rattle of the cot sides penetrated the room below, indicating rest time over and lunch time please, I crept silently up the stairs.

I stood outside his door waiting, and then suddenly I crashed in, making as much noise as I could, and I watched the face in the cot as I crashed. It smiled. There was no surprise, no alarm. I was convinced.

Our GP was reassuring and said that blocked eardrums was quite a common condition in children this age and that he would arrange for us to see the ENT specialist, just to make sure. I was intensely relieved and life took up its old threads again, but Jean and Heather were beginning to get restive and now that Freddy was becoming more mobile and spring was in the air, the garden swing was retrieved from hibernation and tricycles were oiled and pedal cars appeared on the scene and the girls were ready for action. One spring evening they came in from the garden frustrated and despairing. 'Mum,' they said, 'we call him and call him to give him a swing and he just does not answer.' I told them our turn must soon come up for seeing

13

the specialist as five weeks had gone by and then he'd tell us what to do, and begged them to be patient.

We were called to the hospital for an appointment at nine o'clock one morning. I strapped Freddy into the seat on the back of my bicycle and as the family evacuated the house for their schools, Freddy and I set off pedalling our way down the High Street. The waiting room was packed with people and we gave our name to the nurse in charge. She assured us that the very small children would be seen first. I was much relieved and after a trying, wriggling, boring wait of half an hour our name was called. We went into a room I cannot forget. Two doctors in gowns with miners' lamps on their heads were seated on stools. They had a patient each, opposite them on a chair. One of these had his head on one side and a nurse was patting his head as something seemed to be coming out of the lower ear and dropping into a bucket.

We were ushered behind a screen until these two patients were finished with and through the gaping curtains of the screen I could see steam clouding up from a shining fish kettle, and there was an ominous clink of sharp and threatening instruments as they were scissored out of the steam and laid gleaming and ready in kidney basins. There was a short sharp cry from the patient without a bucket, and then it was our turn, and I found my heart thumping wildly and my mouth so dry I could hardly speak. The specialist looked ogre-like with his mouth-mask and his headlamp, but Freddy smiled his fat smile and the specialist's voice was kind. He deftly and speedily went through his tests and at the end of it said 'There is nothing wrong with his eardrums or adenoids, so the child must be deaf. I'll have you see Professor — in Manchester. Next one please.'

I picked up Freddy and we left. There was some card-filling routine to be gone through and then we were outside the hospital and I was strapping him onto the bike again and with cotton-wool knees wove a wobbling way home. I was thinking of everything—I could not think. I asked myself questions. I could not supply the answers. I bundled Freddy into his cot for the morning rest and I picked up the telephone and got through to the specialist's private surgery and made an appointment to see him the next day. When I got there his kind voice said 'Come on in, yes I know, you want to know more. Well of course you do, but you see how it is, we've fifty people to see in one-and-a-quarter hours and it's just not possible. It's health, but it isn't service, now sit down.' He then explained that Manchester University had a research unit for deafness and that it was a world famous clinic and that we would see the best people possible who would be able to tell us more than he could. I thanked him warmly and left and he never sent a bill for his fee.

We then began a waiting time and it was impossible not to watch Freddy's every move and development with this potential hazard in mind. He was growing up fast and becoming interested in string and matchboxes and bricks. He seemed to play intelligently and was self-sufficient.

Every morning when the breakfast had been cleared I stood him on the kitchen table and with one arm firmly round him I pointed through the big window where he could see his father and sisters on their bicycle, fairy cycle and tricycle, pedalling off to their schools. He drummed his feet on the table and waved to them quite wildly and laughed and laughed, and he waited impatiently for this moment every day, squeaking to be lifted onto the table and very anxious not to miss any of it.

For about two months he went through a phase of rushing into the kitchen after his after-breakfast visit to the lavatory, going to the saucepan cupboard under the sink and pulling out every pan and every lid. When these were scattered all round him and he had made certain that all were present and correct, he would begin to cram them all back again. Some of them did not always fit into the cupboard the first time round and the noise was appalling, and he never missed a day, or a pan, while the craze lasted. He would then march purposefully into the nursery —lord of all he surveyed—and make straight for the brick drawer. This was a large drawer and held about a thousand bricks. Some were modern blocks, some were Victorian relics made of black and red and putty-coloured stone and were all sizes including some which were very, very small. Freddy would pull the drawer right out and then, with great difficulty, turn it over, set it to rights and somehow get it back into the chest. It was, needless to say, the bottom drawer. He would then stand in the centre of this sea of bricks with a most satisfied look on his face and feel his day could begin. Sometimes he never touched the bricks all day, but he knew they were there. We had a rigid rule

15

about putting toys away at the end of the day. Freddy needed and got help with his which the girls often thought unfair. Those bricks had us defeated. Even when I dustpanned and brushed them we seemed to crawl around under all the furniture for hours. I felt I had better things to do, so one night I asked my husband to fix a block of wood inside the drawer, preventing it from opening the full pull. Next day, down came Freddy. Into the nursery and out with the drawer. It stuck. He put his head inside, he pulled again, he stood quite still for a few moments staring unbelievingly, and then in what proved later to be typical fashion, he took out the bricks he thought he wanted and settled for the situation.

Life continued, but storm clouds were gathering. Freddy began to know what he wanted and could not tell us. He would start the day with something and then lose it and fail to find it when he remembered it again and cry for we knew not what. I would try to remember what I had seen him with and then look for it, and if by chance I thought I had found it, I would rush to him with a great smile and a 'Here we are' but he would hit it out of my hand and jump up and down and cry more and become enraged and desperate if it wasn't the right thing. The noises he made instead of speech were very upsetting indeed—pleading cries, incessantly repeated and reaching a pitch and volume that jarred our nerves and drove us to try everything we could think of to get him to stop.

After three months we were called to Manchester. It was July, the day dawned and it was raining in that way when you know it's not going to stop—*ever*. It was a very, very long drive to Manchester and Freddy was a creature of habit and he missed his morning rest and his meals were all wrong and he did not like it at all.

My mother came to Manchester from my old home in Yorkshire to hold our hands and it was a joy and a relief to see her and to have someone with us who loved Freddy, but was less emotionally involved and could possibly observe things more objectively. We were in the clinic for a long time. A kind woman sat him down at a child's table. She began by asking me for all the details of the birth and then gave Freddy large jigsaw puzzles to do and other intelligence-test games such as putting wooden wheels with centre holes onto an upright stick and fitting

16

plastic cups inside one another and putting wooden diamond shapes into diamond-shaped spaces. While Freddy was engrossed in his playing, a young girl student walked behind him and made particular noises. Softly at first and then more loudly. He didn't appear to hear those sounds but he was concentrating so hard on his games that we didn't feel he would have heard anything anyway. But who were we to know better than this clinic? It was the best place in the world and we had to keep our thoughts to ourselves, but they did keep nagging. At the end of the afternoon when it was still raining and lights had to be turned on and Freddy was just about played out, the famous Professor came in to see us. He had been assessing the results of the afternoon's tests and he spoke. 'This child is highly intelligent and not deaf, so I advise that you see the best child specialist in the country without delay—good afternoon.'

We were stunned. We had to say goodbye to my mother and I was appalled that we had asked her to come so far only to be plunged further in the dark. The cobbled streets of Manchester between the clinic and the car park were black and oily and the rain ran over them and splashed our summer feet. Freddy was exhausted, disorientated and very upset.

We were icy cold and drove the seemingly endless miles home under a black sky, getting blacker. And for over 200 miles one question stared us in the face. If he isn't deaf then what is it? We found ourselves guiltily wishing he was deaf, as deaf schools are wonderful places today and deaf people even manage to go to universities and get degrees. Very late we collected the girls from friends who had cared for them while we had been away and we thankfully ended our day in the blessed oblivion of sleep.

To wake up with one's mind working from where it left off the night before is an experience known to all, and this became my state for months. Questions and no answers. Our GP was interested but very disappointed with the verdict from Manchester. So was the specialist who really had nothing more to say, but continued to enquire from time to time and to ask us to bring Freddy to see him, always hoping the visit might reveal something. He repeatedly said he had never met anything like it before. Freddy was so sensible and ordered in his behaviour. Certainly he was a slave to routine, but a lot of children are. There were certain things he could not live without, and one was

17

his 'cuddle rug', the remains of a beautiful blue Lanaircel blanket without which he could not sleep and which was the very first thing to be packed if any visits away from home were made. He was using his eyes extensively and noticing things. Winter was coming and my husband would make for the cosy stove when he came in from coaching rugby at his school in the afternoons, riddle and stoke it, and Freddy always accompanied him on these missions and took to laying out all the fire irons in the right order ready for him, but still no speech. The moments of frustration were increasing and there were becoming almost regular sessions about every three days when he failed to find something vital for his life and was unable to tell us.

One day at tea-time Freddy was in his high chair when he suddenly saw something which reminded him of something else. The crying out began, and he had taken to making 'asking' noises. Jean said she had seen him with a match-box in the bathroom and rushed upstairs and returned with it, triumphant. She was met by a face with eyebrows raised in hope and a smile hovering. The ensuing disappointment resulted in a howl of rage and frustration and a hand and arm hit the matchbox away. Heather remembered something in the garden and rushed out for that but with the same result. We then all left the table and searched the house until, at last added to the pile of objects like so much Kim's Game, the cherished thing was found. By this time Freddy was banging his head on the high chair tray in agonies of frustration and crying and throwing himself about, and the rest of us were soon reduced to pieces of chewed string with our nerve-ends jangling and our patience extended to breaking-point. When the treasured object was finally found, the ensuing peace and calm was very alarming and much too un-nerving to be enjoyed. We all knew it would only last until the next time he lost something.

We had come home from Manchester with the phrases 'intelli-gent but not deaf' and 'best child specialist in the country' ringing in our ears and while knowing that something must be done, we found we were strangely reluctant to start any action. I can't ex-plain what it was or why, but I have met many parents of handi-capped children since who have said they experienced the same dis-inclination to push events and would stall and find excuses not to make the required efforts. These efforts involving letters and

18

appointments and interviews were almost more exhausting than the days we were living through and we were overtaken by inertia and let everything slide.

We were well into autumn and my younger sister was to be married in December. This meant a visit to Yorkshire and the excitement of the girls being bridesmaids. We wrote to a doctor practising there who was a distant family connection and whom all my family had always loved and held in high regard. We called him Uncle Arthur. We asked him whom he thought the best child specialist in the country. He wrote back saying he knew, and that he would make all the arrangements for us, and see us at the wedding.

When all the celebrations were safely over we bundled up Freddy, drove to a large hospital in the middle of industry and met Uncle A. He was wonderfully kind. As soon as we saw him we collapsed onto his strength, and he took us to see a paediatrician who had Freddy measured, weighed and put through a number of routine tests. I had to do everything for him under the instructions of a nurse who was irritated not to be allowed to handle him herself. No-one could handle Freddy but me, because he understood nothing that was said, and I had developed a silent communication with him which was made up of special looks, facial expressions, mimes and particularly created atmospheres. The girls had developed a like knack to a lesser but still effective degree, but when it came to making him do things he didn't want to do, it was only I who could manage him. If anybody strange tried to pick him up or even approach him, however gently, it was to him threatening, and his reaction was one of panic. He was almost three years old now and I had never once been away from him. Visits to the hairdresser or any similar activity were unknown in my life at this time, because I could not explain where I was going and, more important, that I would come back. I tried to explain to the offended nurse that he did not understand, but I was wasting my time because she didn't either.

The specialist then ushered us all into another room. It seemed full of people. To begin with there were ourselves and Uncle A, then the redundant nurse, the specialist who went to sit behind a large desk, a stenographer with pencil poised, and about ten postgraduate doctors, sitting-in on the proceedings. Freddy was scrambling about on the floor under the chairs playing with toys provided for the observation, looking very trim in his Chilprufe vest and pants. I had developed clammy hands and a sickening headache and was frightened by what the specialist was going to say and wishing the on-looking and listening doctors and the secretary and nurse would all go away. My husband was sitting as close to me as he could—I knew that so long as he was there I had some hope of holding myself together. Uncle A sat near us, and waves of comfort and strength and reassurance reached us from him. The specialist began, as had the people in Manchester, by asking me for the details of his birth. I reeled off the dramatic saga as quickly as possible wondering why he had not read it in the notes he had about us all. He then asked us questions about Freddy, and all the time he was watching him playing with a train under the chairs. When we seemed to have said everything there was to say he sat back, looked us straight in the eyes, and said that if he was not speaking by the time he was three-and-a-half then he was sorry but we must face the fact that it was most unlikely that he ever would. He went on to say that we must take him upstairs for a head X-ray but that he did not expect to see anything helpful on the picture.

He was as kind as anybody could have been in the circumstances. The postgraduates were staring at their hands and shuffling their feet, the redundant nurse was gazing blankly out of the window and the stenographer was assembling her notes. Blindly, I groped for Freddy under the chairs and rushed out to the ante-room to put on his clothes.

My husband and Uncle A followed and together we stood in the lift which took us up to the X-ray room on the top floor. This room was very large and felt like a planetarium. An efficient sister came up to us, smiled and briskly took Freddy from my arms. There was instant protest, very loud, from him, but nothing compared with what followed when she strapped him on a rubber mat on a steel table and lowered the most terrifying missile very close to his head. I put my fingers in my ears and turned away. We all endured five minutes hell and nobody a worse one than Freddy who was almost hysterical with fright. The sister was understanding and loosened the straps the minute her job was completed. We thanked Uncle A for all his help and most of all his moral support, and we drove away.

We put Freddy to rest when we returned to my parents' home and my mother said she would manage him somehow if he woke up. He had fallen into an instant and deep sleep almost before his head touched the pillow and looked as though he would never wake up. My husband and I drove through the grey December day; we parked our car, walked through heather and looked upon the beautiful winter valley as we tried to see our situation in some sort of perspective. We both began to speak but the sentences never got formed. There were still no answers. We breathed in the thick cold air and returned to the car. The unspoken questions were: What was Freddy's development going to be like without speech? Was anyone going to be able to help him? Were we all going to be able to manage to live with this situation?

I was very distressed to be inflicting such worries and dis-appointments on my parents. They had their own sadnesses and problems but, with their customary generosity and warmth, they took our troubles to the centre of their hearts and backed us up with unrelieved kindness, endless offers of help of every sort, and love. The best of all for us was that they loved and cared about Freddy. If they had shown antipathy towards his condition or resignation I think we should have been done for, for unknow-ingly the fight was on and they were supplying us from the rear.

Acknowledgement that the fight was on came three weeks later when we said to each other, almost simultaneously, 'I don't believe it.' Freddy was at this time saying a sort of 'Mummy' and he had two proper words. One was 'cuckoo' which was for any bird or animal and the other was 'car' which was for anything at all on wheels from a doll's pram to a double-decker bus. This was not much but it was something. It did not fill me with any wild hopes because he still understood nothing in spite of us all talking to him all day long.

It was one thing not to believe it and another to know what to do. In the end my husband wrote to the paediatrician and thanked him for having seen us and said that we simply could not accept his verdict, and was there anything he could suggest? Our GP helped us to elucidate things by explaining that with Freddy's symptoms as they were, he ought to be mentally defective, but as he obviously wasn't, everybody was completely foxed. The ENT specialist with the kind voice was still taking an interest and agreed with the GP saying 'You see, he ought to be mental.' That he wasn't was something so good that we hugged it to ourselves and it was, I suppose, the biggest encouragement in the battle. We received a splendid letter from Yorkshire full of real understanding and saying that two brains were always better than one and giving us an introduction to a friend and colleague in the West.

I did not acknowledge it then, but looking back I believe we refused to accept the situation because I think I knew intuitively that I simply was not up to coping with a speechless child. I think we acted as much from fear of our own inadequacies as for the sake of the child, and no doubt our determination to find a different verdict was in order to relieve us from the feelings of guilt we had about these inadequacies. I can only see this clearly now, for at the time we were in a state of constant fear and dread and much too deeply involved with the situation to be able to analyse our reactions.

We were called to the West in February. Once again arrangements were made for the girls to be looked after and off we went in thick snow. We arrived at the hospital and were shown into a bright room with toys scattered all over the floor. The paediatrician wandered in casually and greeted us. He began by asking for the details of the birth. I took a deep breath and related the events for the third time and I did wonder why notes could not be passed around. He then cast a glance towards Freddy who was wearing a rather smart red sweater, and enquired if this was the child his friend had written the gloomy letter about because he looked 'bright enough' to him. We replied yes, and that though he might look 'bright' he had two words and understood nothing that anyone said. The specialist looked at Freddy and said he couldn't see much wrong and repeated that he looked 'bright enough' to him. We sat mute and there was a long silence broken only by toy-noises going on on the floor. My husband asked what one did about children who did not speak or understand. He didn't seem to know and then a woman doctor came in and we were introduced and the specialist explained the situation implying that he could not really understand why we had come as the child seemed so 'bright' to him. In the nick of time my husband put out a restraining hand. I believe he knew that there was real and imminent danger of a flying handbag.

Tears of desperation were stinging the edges of my eyes and I didn't like the emotions I was having. This man was not acknowledging a situation of a speechless, non-comprehending child with a future we had to face. He was just standing there saying he 'seemed' bright and I knew if he said it again I would hit him. The deadlock was resolved when he said Freddy must go into the next room and see the psychiatrist! I laughed. But I led him in. I was extremely curious to see what would happen.

Freddy was spoken to by a sombre man with brown eyes who, when no response was forthcoming, gave him some beads to thread. While this was happening my husband in the other room was asking the woman doctor what one did with non-comprehending, speechless children and she remarked that there was a special school for children with speech difficulties in the South. My husband immediately asked where it was and what it was called and how one got there. It was an independent school run by a board of managers but with fees paid by local education authorities. Freddy and the psychiatrist and I came in through the door just as the specialist was saying 'Oh, they'd never have him *there,* he's far too bright.' I clutched my bag in one hand and held on to Freddy with the other but my head began to throb like an all-time hangover and I knew that it was better to be in a deep snowdrift all night than stay in that place another second.

We skidded and slithered our way home but my husband had the address of the special school safely tucked away in his breast pocket and a promise from the woman doctor to write to them and arrange for us to go and see them. Next day he wrote to her and asked for confirmation in writing that this would happen and he received a reply to the effect that we would be sent for some time in the summer. Brown envelopes in the post had always been unwelcome, but now they were the first thing we looked for.

Spring came and went and everyone had chicken-pox. Freddy was evolving a strange language of his own and he actually began to say the girls' names, or a version of them, but it was pure chance if he put the right name to the right girl. The reaction of people we knew was interesting. Some quite obviously reckoned we'd got an appalling problem and were loath to talk about it preferring to wish it just wasn't happening. All this with very kind looks and all manner of touching gestures. A large number were impatient with us and flatly denied there could be anything wrong, rightly observing that Freddy did exactly what I told him, therefore of course he understood. I was feeling particularly vulnerable one day when a friend was expressing these views in a hard voice, and I turned on her and explained that I had trained Freddy as one trains an intelligent gun dog and that we didn't need words and that one look from me would release wireless knobs from fingers and have books replaced on shelves, but that actually saying it produced a blank. 'You'll see,' she insisted, 'he'll suddenly say everything' and then I had to listen to interminable tales of children who had not said a word until they were five, six, and even seven.

These were occasions when I came very near to throwing things again and suffered tortures of frustration because I was always hoping people would understand the problem as we knew it. If they were thinking of Freddy, then their theories were not helpful to him. No-one could understand Freddy unless they lived with him. Kind and sympathetic and generous and long-suffering as so many of our friends were, outside my family my greatest source of comfort and relief was in fact our daily, Mrs Cornock. She was quiet and kind and balanced. She cared very much about Freddy. She never tried to know better than us and I bless her for the *hours* she clocked up over twelve years with us, spent listening to me talking out my thoughts and struggling. Freddy grew in confidence with her. She came twice a week and made the house gleam, and as she never let me down and never seemed to be ill, Freddy relied upon this splendid relationship which was such an addition to his security. He never attempted her name, but I rejoiced to see him welcome her with recognition and I could leave him with her without a qualm for pressing engagements like the dentist.

The best friends were the ones who recognized a problem, asked us straight what was going to happen and admitted it was all very strange and bewildering. Sympathy was always touching and warming but what one craved was understanding. The future was too frightening to contemplate, but it was going to come and my relentless line of insisting on seeing things exactly

24

as they were in every context often made people think that I
was wallowing in pessimism and refusing encouragement. I
could not get excited when Freddy added a few odd words to
his vocabulary because there was still no communication and,
anyway, in order to survive I was not risking disappointment. All
the same we were at war, struggling to find an answer and in
our innermost recesses we had to have hope.

In May a sister-in-law came to stay, with her son Jim, who
was the same age as Freddy. Her husband had been posted
abroad and she could not accompany him because she was
threatened with a miscarriage. It was horrible for her and we
were very sorry for her, especially as she had to go to bed and
stay there from the moment she arrived. Life became hectic.
Freddy and his cousin were practically twins and there were
terrible fights over tricycles and tin cars. There were meals to be
taken upstairs, Jean and Heather's school affairs, and two boys
to bath. I said to my husband before they came that this could
be good and that maybe Freddy would start talking like the
cousin. I mentioned earlier that he was evolving his own
language and one word he would say at this time was 'kekie'.
This was an asking word and he would say it with a question
mark and his hands outstretched. Freddy and Jim had eyed one
another silently on meeting and then settled for cautious play.
As they got used to each other the intensity of the good times
and the fights increased, and then one day my sister-in-law had
finally to go to hospital.

Freddy was enjoying company. One sunny morning I was
busy in the kitchen and the boys were meant to be playing in
the garden. I heard the patter of bare feet in the hall and a voice
calling 'Kekie? Kekie?' I ran out, all ready to try to find out
what Freddy wanted, to be met by Jim. He had Freddy's
intonation perfected. I felt wild with rage. What hope was there
for man ever to progress? Why did we bother with attempting to
be civilized? I calmed myself and kissed Jim and asked him
what he wanted, still hoping to solve the mystery of 'kekie' as
we had none of us managed to discover what it meant. Of
course he didn't know, or wouldn't tell, and I sent him back into
the garden to play. When my husband came in from school
that day I greeted him with the story. 'Can you beat it?' I
asked. 'Some hope of Freddy learning anything from Jim, it's

25

the other way round and he is speaking like Freddy' and I was crying tears of anger and disappointment as I had pinned so much hope on results from communication with this boy of identical age. At first he could not believe it and then he laughed and went out and bought a bottle of whisky and poured me out a large one and it did me a lot of good.

In July we were called to the special school for an interview. What were we to do with Jim? His mother was still away in hospital, there was no-one we knew well enough to risk leaving him with, and no-one he knew. Three years old is not an easy age and he just had to come with us. In the end my mother-in-law came to our rescue and after making the old arrangements for the girls, we set off in our new Bedford van for the South. We met Granny and she coped with Jim while we went to the school.

Once again the icy fear began to creep through our veins. This time it was not so much what they were going to tell us about Freddy but whether they were going to take him at the school. Goodness knows we did not want to send him away from home but if they didn't have him, who would and what would happen? When we arrived we were introduced to a pleasant woman who took him off to a room for some intelligence tests. They seemed to consist of the jigsaws and puzzles he had done in Manchester and I noticed the beads to be threaded like the ones the psychiatrist had given him. That done, we were taken into a very small room full of people. There was an elderly doctor and some speech therapists. Everyone was in gleaming white overalls and everyone was talking. We sat down and I was asked to give them the details of the birth. I longed to say that surely they had sent them from the West, if not Yorkshire or even Manchester, but it seemed best just to recount the saga yet again and I had it off pat by then. The doctor looked at Freddy and picked him up and sat him on his knee. He turned over the pages of a nursery book and the pictures were large and simple, of animals and objects. To my consternation Freddy said 'Cuckoo' loud and clear at the picture of a bird and I thought that we were done for and they would think he was all right and send us away. After about ten minutes when the doctor had asked us a lot of questions about his behaviour and habits and general state, he turned to us and said

'This is a straightforward case of aphasia and he must come to us when he is five.'

For a brief moment we were quite stunned. We could not believe our ears. Somebody knew what was wrong and had a place where it could be put right. The relief was so intense that I indulged in a moment of being sorry for myself because it was going to be so awful sending him away. This was luxury. A voice was cutting in on those wild thoughts and giving us some information.

We were told that aphasia had only recently been discovered, that it was a condition still not recognized by a lot of doctors and one that was very rare. The translation of the original Greek is literally 'no speak', but the general use includes non-understanding as well. The doctor said it was caused by a shortage of cells in the brain which stored words. He asked searching questions about the girls and the ages at which they spoke and on hearing that they were quite normal went on to say that it amounted to nothing really as the condition was far more prevalent in boys. He also observed that speech defects of every kind, particularly stuttering, are more prevalent in males than females. He stated categorically that the condition was not hereditary, but was familial, and implied that this meant something to do with genes and that we were bad at making boys. Being wholly committed to his research he asked hopefully if we were expecting or intending any more children, and for the purposes of his research it would have suited him splendidly if we had another son like Freddy. We had hoped for a fourth child but nothing had come of it, and after the results of this interview I didn't relish the idea of producing babies to have them sent away at five, and we did not have any more.

Although Freddy had suffered brain damage at birth through too much oxygen being given—the only known way of keeping premature babies alive at that time—and bad jaundice, the doctor said he knew of cases similar to Freddy's where the birth had been quite normal. We found we could be objectively interested in all this because we were not in the least concerned about cause, only effect, and what could be done about it. It is good to know that premature babies are now given something in addition to oxygen since it was discovered that oxygen on its own was a cause of brain damage. Freddy was born just too soon for that, but one is sure to be too late or too soon for something and this was Freddy's lot so when brain damage was mentioned we just said a prayer of gratitude as we felt that, with anything as delicate as a brain, all the things we had probably narrowly missed did not bear contemplating.*

The doctor said: 'You realize that this boy is one of six known children in the British Isles?' It was strangely exhilarating to hear that Freddy was so special, so exclusive, and it seemed that it justified something. These vain thoughts were quickly nettled by a still small voice from within which gave out a warning that to be medically interesting was one thing, but to get your rarity fitted into life was quite another.

We then asked if there was anything we could do to help while we waited the eighteen months till he was school age. There were three things. When he was four we were to install some resident help so that he could get used to other people handling him, go to the Municipal offices and register for some speech therapy, and introduce him to a nursery school to get him used to children in numbers. Late in the afternoon and armed with these marching orders we left. We knew we must be the luckiest people alive.

* For further information about aphasia, see the Note by Pauline Griffiths at the end of this book.

28

2

Freddy found it a tremendous effort to keep up with life each day. It was a strain which seemed to be mental and which reacted on him physically. If bedtime was not at 5.30 sharp, he was almost asleep on his feet. One very hot day that summer, friends had come to play tennis. We had just managed to squeeze a court onto the garden and though it was home-made and hazardous it was a lot of fun. The guests lingered on and I found it was after 6 pm and very late for Freddy. I excused myself and went in search of him. He was nowhere to be found. The girls were busy climbing trees and had not seen him for some time. With a pounding heart I ran to the front, but the gate was firmly latched. I went indoors and searched every room. No Freddy. I began to look in ridiculous places. It was never any use calling. I ran outside again and walked right round the house. There, on the north side, lying fast asleep on a cold stone slab in the shade of a big tree, was Freddy. He had even gone upstairs and collected his cuddle-rug; he really was the most sensible little boy. The heatwave continued and some days later when the garden was full of children, we had all had a game of hide and seek. Again it was after 5.30 and Freddy came up to me, took me by the wrist, led me into the house, up the stairs, into the bathroom and then he pulled my arm forward and placed my hand on a tap. I acted promptly and bathed him immediately. It was good living with someone who knew when he had had enough.

Jim left. His mother was better and the two of them flew away to foreign parts. Freddy did not seem to notice that he had gone. Summer holiday time came round and as he was three-and-a-half we decided he was old enough to be taken camping. The special school people had recommended making life interesting and stimulating so off we went to spend our first night on a friend's farm in Shropshire. It poured with rain and we woke up to flapping canvas and a dreadful dampness. The girls were in a tent together and we had Freddy in with us. I dressed him and put on his gumboots and he staggered over our bed to investigate the outside. He pushed aside the canvas flap and a great gust of wind blew him straight back in. His expression was one of disconcerted surprise and served as an adequate initiation to years of camping holidays. We continued in bad weather to the Lakes. The rain and gales made it impossible for any real enjoyment and the last straw was a trip on Lake Windermere in a pleasure boat which had window-wipers in perpetual motion.

All this time Freddy was still suffering wild and terrible moments of frustration and rage. The girls were so good. Jean had the patience of Job, a staggering, unselfish, long-suffering patience, and endlessly and tirelessly fetched and carried for him and played with him. Heather had the capacity to make him laugh. She could be droll, and he appreciated this. He was a lucky boy; in his sisters he had got everything. It was trying for them. The dolls' house was often wrecked and precious things mislaid and they could never ask him where he had put them. At times like this camping holiday, he would get bored with the journey and noisy when he was tired and we all had days when we felt impotently exhausted, emotionally, physically, mentally. He struggled to be included, the lack of speech communication taxed our imaginations, and when we got irritated and impatient I became acutely aware how hard it was on the girls and wondered if I should spare them. We were a family and we all belonged.

We had decided some time previously that we must approach the Church to see if they could help Freddy, but it seemed hardly fair until we had a clear-cut problem to present. We knew so much more after our visit to the special school that the time seemed to have come. Some time before our camping holiday one of the Mirfield Fathers had come down to preach in our town and had called on us. He promised to think about our problem, and three weeks after this visit he had sent us the name of an old priest living in Cornwall who had devoted the last twenty years of his life to the study and practice of spiritual healing. We had been in touch with this man and he and his wife kindly asked us to stay during our holidays. We decided we would rather be on our own so, after drying out our tents at my parents' home to which we had thankfully retreated after the Lakes, we left the girls on their farm and packing the largest tent, set off for the wilds.

I felt very nervous and thoroughly apprehensive about this strange pilgrimage but I also felt certain we were going to see someone to whom we could hand over all our doubts and fears. And indeed we could. The priest and his wife were kindly and welcoming. They appreciated our wishes for privacy and offered us the vicarage airing cupboard for wet clothes. They showed us a field at the back of their house and we laid the groundsheet on rich lush sodden grass and rigged the tent in record time against sheeting rain. Freddy watched everything from the Bedford van and showed excitement when he saw his cot mattress going in. Once he was safely fed and bedded down we settled ourselves with sherry in tin mugs and some hot stew and it all felt very strange in our cocoon world with flickering candles, the incessant drumming of rain on the canvas and the shivering damp.

I made some coffee and then my husband struggled into his gumboots and disappeared into the night for the first of the talks with the priest. I looked at our son asleep on his mattress in the middle of nowhere and I was not sure who I was, what I was doing or why.

We awoke to the same sound to which we had fallen asleep. Rain, steady, relentless, wet, wet rain. Everything in our tent was clammy. My clothes as I put them on felt wringing, and the sugar was solid, the bacon had gone slimy and the butter was hard and very cold. Hot tea helped, and then we woke Freddy. He was taking camping in his stride by this time; it was something you did when it poured with rain. That morning he and his father went off for a look at the sea and I went to the vicarage. We had decided to see the priest separately. First, because Freddy could not be left, and secondly because I knew that my husband and the priest would be speaking to each other on an infinitely higher intellectual plane than I could manage. I went in and sat down and nobody asked me to give them the details of the birth. I said straight away that I was not at all sure that I wasn't there under false pretences and that if he held his healing service and Freddy immediately spoke I should run a mile. He was a most understanding man and said it would be abnormal not to be feeling as I was and then tried to explain what it was all about. I understood every word he said at the time and I liked him very much. By the time I was standing on the front doorstep and saying goodbye it had all gone. But I was prepared to take things on trust and I embarked on painting the woodwork in our spare bedroom when we returned home, and while scraping away at the panels of the old shutters, all the priest had told me began to make itself plain in digested form.

Cud-chewing must have been going on in the dark recesses of my brain and this uninterrupted spell of paint working was just what was needed for proper appreciation. If it was just healing that we were after, then we were wanting the wrong things. Ten lepers were healed but the one who ran back and thanked Christ was made whole. It was to be made whole in spite of; it was being acceptable and accepting even if limbs or eyes were missing, this was the aim, and on the second morning of our stay in Cornwall we woke to a clear fresh quiet sky.

We went to the eleventh-century church, a perfect specimen of its kind. The priest's wife had put country garden flowers on the altar and the stone walls and oak pews were mellow, solid and unquestionable. A few local worshippers had responded to a small notice in the porch, a convent of nuns who specialize in prayers for healing were with us in spirit, and also several friends and family of our own. After an ordinary Communion service, we three remained at the altar rails and the priest blessed some oil which he had in an oyster shell and he simply and swiftly anointed Freddy and said a small prayer. We returned to our tent, made some breakfast, packed ourselves up, said our fare-wells and set off home.

It was September and I was busy getting out the winter clothes. We had told only one local friend about our pilgrimage as we felt certain that most people would find it all rather embarrassing. I had myself been embarrassed to begin with. As life resumed its threads and various friends brought their children to tea, three of them made the same but separate observation that Freddy seemed 'quite different' since the summer. When anyone said that, then, of course, we told them where we had been, and sure enough his troubles may not have been over but we never had any more frustration incidents. Freddy had received some sort of peace. Never again did he bang his head on the table but from that time seemed able to accept himself, and the rest of us found we were the more able to accept the situation.

A writers' conference took place in our town that autumn and we were asked to give two women writers accommodation. In contrast to his complete indifference to casual callers Freddy was very intrigued by the ladies from London. Each morning that week at nine, he marched along to the spare room. They kindly invited him in to their fruit and coffee breakfasts. They had, in fact, no choice! But they made him welcome and communication developed between them involving a head and hand gesture which became a ritual. He seemed to need to be involved with people and we were thankful he showed tendencies to be extrovert rather than introvert.

And then he was four and life began to get earnest. We found a nursery school, we found some mother's help, and speech therapy was arranged for once a week. These were a lot of happenings all at once but we reckoned Freddy must learn to take it. He was very apprehensive about speech therapy and he and I descended to the basement of the municipal buildings and I sat with him on my knees and the speech therapist chatted to him and showed him her books and equipment. It was many weeks before I was able to leave hir happily with her alone and it was for short spells at first, and two months before we could all manage the whole half hour with confidence.

It was the same with nurser school. The first day I took him, we sat together on a tiny chair and observed everything for twenty minutes. Freddy clung to me and his eyes watched for my every move. The next four days we repeated this, sitting a while longer each time. On the fifth day I put him down, the nursery school teacher gave him a book and I left the room for six minutes. He rushed at me when I returned. The next week I put him straight into the room and left him for ten minutes. All was well. Thirty minutes, an hour, and we were there. Once he cottoned on and saw that I always came for him at the end of the session, he began to enjoy the nursery school. He was happy and energetic and he even began riding to school on his tricycle with me or the 'help' beside him in the gutter on my old bicycle.

The 'helps' (there were three in that year) at first seemed disastrous. One only took the job to be near her man friend and he wouldn't have her so she left. The second left because her man would have her. The last three months of the year a young cousin came to fill in time before going to Kenya. She was splendid. As each of the others gave notice my heart sank as I felt the chopping and changing would be upsetting for Freddy, but as it turned out it was quite a good thing and a lesson in self-reliance. I think he found the changes stimulating, but as with Jim, he made no deep attachments and did not seem to notice when they left. But I did, and as the end of the year came in sight I knew that parting with him was going to be impossible and that no-one was going to understand about him and yet at the same time that some life without him was going to give us all a much needed break.

We had to do all Freddy's thinking for him. His every need had to be anticipated. He had no sense of time and we could not enjoy holiday planning and packing with him, we could not warn him that his birthday or anyone else's was coming. We just had to wake up one morning and 'have' Christmas day. He was saying a few more words but he did not know who he was or where he lived. One phrase he did say was 'Happy Day'. He would say this at the end of the day. It became a 'time' thing, and was associated with that particular moment. He did not know what he was saying.

We had to be very careful never to lose Freddy. The ENT specialist had warned us that when he was four his tonsils and adenoids would have to come out. Fortunately we contributed to BUPA and so could choose a time that suited us and he went into a nursing home where I could be with him right up to the moment of oblivion and as soon as he 'came round'. I could not warn him of hyperdermic needles or soften the blow as to how he would feel after the operation and for three days it was just a question of reassurance by presence. The surgeon told the nursing staff about his condition, but it never made sense to people, and as they dutifully replied 'Yes doctor' I knew that they had not registered what they had been told and sure enough when their coaxings and cajolings were rejected they lost patience, then interest. When we left the home it was the girls' half-term, and I took the three of them in an old-fashioned way for a long weekend in Bournemouth.

We camped in Skye that summer and we spent some days in Northumberland with a large gathering of clans on our way up there. I was secretly dreading this. I knew that Freddy would not be able to keep up, that his routine would go for six, that he would get no pleasure from his contemporary cousins and that the family would be kind, concerned but baffled and I just didn't want to talk about it. Sure enough, at 5.30 we would still be on the beach but Freddy would want only to be in bed, he was having a bad spell of not enjoying food and hotels are terrifying places if children are being finnicky. We all went off to the Farne Islands and he was terrified of the big waves, our fishing smack ferry and the circling birds. I held him close and firm but he wasn't to be pacified. It was no good, a large family party just wasn't his thing and it was with some relief that we retreated into our own family unit again, re-packed the trailer and headed for Scotland.

This family only had to put up one tent and rain would come down. Six out of seven days we saw Skye through swirling rain clouds. Gumboots were wetter inside than out, the children made shell-collections shrouded in macs and rain hats. The sugar was solid again and the endless patient reminders from my husband not to touch the tent sides worked up to phrenetic screamings by the end of the week. He is a very peaceloving, patient man and generally stolid in adversity, but on one of these days which seemed to be wetter than any day we had ever known, I slithered and sloshed my way on sea-grass and streaming clay to the small clearing we had made among the gorse bushes and found him there on our thunderbox, under an enormous old Cambridge-days umbrella which had large drops of rain falling from its beaded points, gazing hopelessly across the Atlantic. The picture was complete in its total resignation, a 'cartoon' of typical British Summer Holidays. I called to him : 'Cheer up, it can't get any worse!' I was laughing, 'Get your resistance down . . .' After that, we gave ourselves over to the elements and suddenly everything became more bearable, but only just, and we ended the holiday with three dry days in Edinburgh, where Freddy was thrilled with the pipe band which paraded down Princes Street each morning at eleven in honour of the Edinburgh Festival. The wind blew, the sun shone, we met old friends and remembered the holiday for a long time afterwards as being terrific.

Autumn came and went, then a happy Festive Yorkshire Christmas. Freddy lived in his own world with his new Christmas toys, loving being with the girls, which was not always fair on them, and noisily and unintelligibly making his presence felt.

He did not know this was the end of such security for ever.

3

It was now time for Freddy to go to the special school. The school where the interview had taken place eighteen months previously had changed its policy, and the present arrangement was that the five-to-nine-year-olds attended the John Horniman School, which was administered by the Invalid Children's Aid Association and was recognized by the Department of Education and Science as a boarding special school for children suffering from speech and language disorders.

My husband was taking a party of schoolboys on a skiing expedition; I had encouraged him to do so. Leaving the girls in Yorkshire, I packed the cuddle-rug, and Freddy and I set off to Granny's. We stayed the night with her and next day as she saw us off, we could not speak. There was everything and nothing to say. I think that Freddy knew there was something up. He sat very still in the Bedford van and was quite unusually silent.

Freddy walked in through the door and knew. He was very upset. He cried. The boilerman was asked to take him with him to watch while he mended a fuse. I was introduced to the speech therapist and together we discussed Freddy in detail. I had previously written to the matron telling her how I had settled him at nursery school and begging her to let us come down and stay in a nearby hotel, guaranteeing to have Freddy peacefully installed within ten days. This request was flatly refused. I tried to compose myself as I explained the situation to the speech therapist and told her I knew the matron would eventually find she had never met a child like this before, by which time it would all be too late. She was very sympathetic but left the place at the end of the day and had nothing to do with the administrative resident staff. The headmistress was a person full of energy and purpose. She had never handled children like this before and she was looking forward to discoveries with determination and professional anticipation. I was sent away and told to return at four to say goodbye to Freddy. I could hear him crying desperately in the distance but I had to do what I was told. I left the school and walked blindly into the grey January day.

I wandered along the deserted sea front enduring my impotence. Every clock in the town had been fixed, the minutes did not pass. I never drink gin but I went into a restaurant bar and drank three John Collins. With each one I hoped for the unfreezing of my heart and mind, but nothing happened at all and attempting escape from Freddy's crying, I bought a bath bun and walked the length of the pier, hoping the noise of the waves and the gulls would drown the other. The pier was deserted, the executioner's chopper was poised, frozen over the little wooden head of Mary the Queen, all the things the butler saw were waiting dustily to be seen again, the robot-like faces on the football men and jockeys were in compulsory hibernation until the spring, the rusty hinges on the boarded sweet booths rattled and a thin dog whimpered in a busy restless searching this way and that across the oily planks. I hung over the railings, which needed new paint, and gazed down at the onyx sea as it sloshed round the piers and over the ochre shingle. Freddy was alone and we were all powerless to help him. I could not argue my point because authority had its point too and we were lucky to have found this place and in it were contained all our hopes.

I burned with bitter resentment for this senseless ordeal. It could only do damage. I dug my hands deep into my pockets and set off towards the town. Freddy's birthday was two weeks off so I ordered a cake. I had time to shop, time I had not had for five years. I saw household things I knew we needed but when it came to buying them I turned away telling myself we could manage without, and then without warning I was overtaken by a compulsion to choose and buy a hideous knitting-bag which I knew I didn't need and would never use. A lift flew me up two floors to a café where I drank some tea I did not want and then mercifully and sickeningly someone had set the clocks working again because the hands said half past three. If I had walked backwards and blindfold I could not have taken half an hour for the return journey from the shops to the school, yet there I was flustering with my purse to pay for the tea, scrambling through the little tables and rushing down the stairs, too impatient to wait for lifts. At 3.40 I was back and Freddy was rushing at me crying over and over again 'Happy Day, Happy

38

Day.' His face was blotched red-white-blue and he was quivering with exhaustion. I told them he must be put to bed and that he always had a banana which might help. I was not allowed to do this myself and they said it would be better if I went.

There was no way of telling him that I had not left him for life. I went to a gloomy hotel for the night and I couldn't eat and the clocks had stopped again. I wrote a dreadful letter to my parents and felt treacherous next day when it was irrevocably on its way. Had I exploited Freddy's dilemma and indulged in melodramatic self-pity? I had been searching for relief and there was none. Next morning I telephoned the school and they said he had slept and was all right. I believed them because I had to and I set off the 130 miles home.

We lived and worked like automata until the weekend we were allowed to go and take him out. Forty miles from the town, Red Queen like, I shouted 'Faster, faster, faster' and we did arrive. I was out of the van before it had stopped and into the Matron's waiting room where we were kept for an interview before being allowed to see Freddy. She was vaguely reassuring, very puzzled by him, kind in a practical way. Suddenly he was there, led in by a house mother. He scrambled onto my knee and clung like a monkey. We drove to Granny where a welcome awaited us, crackling fires, comfortable chairs, toys for Freddy and splendid food. He never uttered a sound all day and wanted only to sit on my knee. The clock people had been at their tricks again and this time the hands were whirling round in double time. Freddy couldn't eat, but as he looked quite well we didn't worry. Suddenly we all knew it was at an end and we had to return and put him back again. I cuddled him through the traffic, half praying for a breakdown, a puncture, any hazard to prevent the inevitable. We all went in, the staff on duty greeted Freddy with earthquaking cheerfulness, he went with them, mutely, in resignation and we returned home.

There were two visiting weekends each term, and our second one was a repetition of the first. There was a breath of spring in the air and I revelled in the thought that the third time we went down it would be to collect him and bring him home. Thinking of the surprise he would get was so good that this kept us going till that blessed day. It came, in spite of the clock people, and this time we had long talks with the teacher and the speech

39

therapist. They were fascinated by Freddy and had both developed bonds of communication with him. This was wonderful news. My heart warmed to the house mothers who meant so well and were so kind and cheerful. Everybody was lovely that day. We were going home.

Freddy's case, cuddle-rug still intact, but only just, and safely packed, was put in the van, and then he clambered onto my knee and we were off. He saw his home and he clapped his hands. Jean and Heather rushed out as they had the day he came home from hospital. A moment passed faster than lightning when I noticed a fleeting expression of envy on the face of the elder girl. She had always harboured dramatic fantasies about herself at boarding schools! We all went in. I watched Freddy surveying the hall, the nursery, the kitchen and his room.

All the holiday he was subdued, very clinging and inclined to tears. We organized as many adventures as possible. All attempts to keep up acquaintance with other children his own age became too difficult as they were all striding ahead in good five-year-old fashion, and the hazards of non-comprehension and non-communication were being realized. He was small and this was a help in one way as people in general did not guess his age and made allowances. He still got the girls' names wrong. We had not expected a dramatic change in him and we did not get it. He always came to church with us for the early services, and joined us at the altar for a blessing. He was always happy doing this and it was a life line for us. That was his first school holiday. It was over and we set off again. Freddy knew as well as we when we were nearing the end of the journey and the Red Queen was not with us but we arrived just the same. We clambered out of the van and it was impossible to tell if the welcome given Freddy by the staff did anything for him. He turned from us scarlet, and let himself be led away. We had a brief word with the matron about the dentist and other practicalities and braced ourselves for our return. We bolstered ourselves with the encouraging thought that maybe Freddy with his sensibility now knew that he did come home and that when this had happened once more, he would relax.

Letters from school arrived. About six assorted capital letters copied from the board, kisses larger than the paper they were written on and various crude drawings. We sent picture post-cards every week. My mood decided the choice of these. Some-times they were from the Beatrix Potter books, often I found beautiful cards of kittens, horses or dogs, and occasionally I sent Van Goghs, Monets and other impressionists, rather aggressively as a counter-action to Noddy and all the plastic toys.

The matron had found out for herself that Freddy could not last out until the official bedtime and he was having a personal routine. We were delighted, and there were other signs of flexibility, as the staff came to understand how uniquely diverse and complex all the children were. They were full this term, and for the rest of Freddy's time there, with twenty-four pupils. They all had a communication problem in common but each was affected in a different way. The head teacher's ingenuity was put to olympian tests and the way she adapted her methods to suit each individual child was a feat which would have daunted most people in the profession. She never ceased thinking of ways round the children's problems and it was her endless infectious encouragement and enthusiasm which got Freddy hooked on learning.

That summer we camped dryly but without sun in Norfolk on a friend's farm. We had a girl cousin with us, and the farmer had four children. Each day we exchanged a child for lunch, so there was a constant variety of company, and that, coupled with a swimming pool in the garden and intriguing barley- and pea-harvesting in progress, made a stimulating and educative break. Freddy took a great interest in everything that was happening. We spent one breezy bright day at the sea and bathed and his previous fear of the waves seemed to have disappeared.

Leaves were turning, we needed our gumboots as we tramped for water in the early morning dew and the magical tang we caught in the evening air told us that summer was over bar the blackberries.

That winter term he took his tricycle with him. There was a splendid yard and wheeled vehicles were encouraged. The loaded silence that fell between us all from the moment the car set off spoke of unbreakable bonds of unquestioned love and mutually inarticulate understanding. When we arrived he once again turned, scarlet in the face, and walked straight through the door, indifferent to the off-loading of paraphernalia.

It was a source of interest, relief and some pride to us that he

41

did not suffer from the nervous reactions so common to children under strain. No bitten nails and never a wet bed.

The term went well and our visits, though subdued and lunchless, were more bearable. We were indescribably indebted to our Granny for living where she did and providing a haven. Our hearts went out to the less fortunate parents eking out the long days in cafés and on deserted piers or in unsuitable cinemas. School had a party and a Father Christmas and then it was time to assess the end of the first year. Speech was progressing. There was quite a vocabulary. About thirty words, including his name and recognizable names of the staff.

Time, of which he still had no sense, passed. Another birthday cake was organized and small presents for everybody, to help towards the party the school held on birthdays.

It was at the end of this spring term that conclusions were drawn, from various coincidences, that Freddy was deaf to some degree. The speech therapist was the main detector and she was convinced of this new condition from particular observations she had made.

Tests were undergone at a clinic during the holidays which ascertained a marked high frequency hearing loss. It didn't seem possible that Manchester could have made a mistake, but apparently they had, and as it turned out, a good mistake because if Freddy had been diagnosed deaf and sent to one of their schools, the teaching methods would not have been effective in view of his aphasic condition and it seemed there could only have ensued muddle and misunderstanding, and finally a painful change.

We found ourselves pinning great hopes on the little box which now lodged in his breast pocket, with its delicate flex to the ear-plug. The Hoover being turned on without warning provoked Freddy to expertise with the 'on' and 'off' knob, and we were forever catching him with it off. The instrument increased all sound, what he heard as well as what he didn't and we all became conscious of hearing hazards we had previously never thought about. Heavy lorries passed in the street and his hand would fly to that tiny knob. It was the same with low-flying aircraft, slamming doors and opera singers on the radio. We had to be fierce about its being kept on and his getting used to it, or things weren't going to improve, and there was a constant battle about it. The aid obviously was one, but effort was required of him, more than he was prepared to make. We had discovered one of his bolt holes. Not hearing became a great escape, and a temporary answer when life became difficult and it almost continuously was. We soon realized how much we were going to have to be on our guard to prevent Freddy from opting out into deafness.

Having a hearing aid he had to wear all the time was just one more hazard for Freddy to cope with. The tiny batteries did not last long; the flex was so fine that it quickly and easily wore out. He was self-conscious about the look of the instrument and always showed great delight if it went away for repairs and was a long time returning.

He was now six-and-a-quarter and when people asked what was wrong and just what 'aphasic' meant, I told them that aphasia for Freddy seemed to be an appreciation of some situations but a non-comprehension of the meaning of words, which, with the added complication of hearing loss, made communication difficult and complicated.

It was about this time that Tanya entered our lives, a Russian who had married a British war correspondent after being his secretary in Moscow during the war. At this time she was acting as publicist for a newly formed theatre ballet company and came to our town as advance guard with information. Various members of the community got together to see how best to promote and help this enterprise. It was decided that free hospitality should be offered to all the dancers. Tanya had a Russian daughter by a previous marriage, Anna, who had escaped to the free world and was dancing with the company. Anna and Tanya took up residence with us.

Thus a most happy and, for us, unique and unusual week began. I seemed to do nothing but cook large steaks. The dancers expended a fantastic amount of energy and steak was the only hope of keeping them successfully on their feet. The nursery was littered with discarded ballet shoes in every shade from bottle green to conventional pink. There was something infinitely touching and nostalgic about the pink ones. They lasted no time at all and it was impossible to throw them out; they had danced, and it would have been like discarding an old violin.

43

' Each morning the girls were waiting with intense excitement to collect these treasures and stuff them with cotton wool in an endeavour to make them fit. Every moment was spent on points and they were temporarily transported into secret worlds of dancing dreams and dreams of dancing.

One day Anna asked me if the children would like to join her for a rehearsal. The girls could not believe she meant it, but she did, and off they went to the theatre. Three small stools were placed down stage left, and on them sat the girls and Freddy. Their eyes never left the steaming dancers as they went through their bar work and flung themselves into their pirouettes, leaps and turns. My family returned home with sparkling eyes, inspired. Freddy marched into the nursery, went straight to the corner where the girls had their treasures hoarded in a box and selected a pair of black shoes. His small feet slipped straight to the end of the blocks leaving an empty shoe-horn effect sticking out at the back, but nothing daunted he wound the ribbons round his legs, indicated that help was required for tying them securely at the ankles and then he was off. His arms shot stiffly upwards in his Fair Isle jersey and he proceeded with determination to attempt a turn on points. He was very clumsy, but he kept at it and this craze for dancing was the lasting theme for the holidays.

The following term some fun began with the boilerman taking the boys from the school to the local boys' club gymnasium. Once each week they went off in the school bus and this was a very popular move, especially with Freddy who went mad about the trampoline. Not only was there a gym-club social before Christmas, but there were boys from the club in these gym classes and it was very good for them all to be meeting each other and having to mix and manage with the minimum allowances made.

The people who make the policy for special schools are aware that they are unavoidably hot-houses. It is very difficult to achieve self-reliance in children from such schools—they cannot be protected for ever yet they need protection. The ideal school is one where the disabled take part in all the general activities such as gym, art and singing but are streamed off to special classes within the unit according to needs. I am sure it is only a question of time before such integrated schooling will exist and be taken for granted. The degree of disability suffered by Freddy and his colleagues was so great that it was impossible to imagine them being successful in such a set-up at this stage, but it was the kind of thing to which one hoped they would graduate, rather than stay for all their schooling in a wholly understanding community which was going to have to spill them into an un-understanding and possibly hostile world at the end of it all.

Freddy was slowly accumulating scattered fragments of information. These fragments were fine in themselves but seemed to exist in isolated irrelevance in his mind. The head teacher began enterprising projects and there would be an introduction to a subject with pictures, photographs and talk, building up to a great day when a visit was made to the chosen subject and everything studied was seen to be real, followed by a conclusion when drawings were expected of what had been seen. There were projects on bread, and the post office, the harbour, and wool. Then came the garage. This was situated opposite the school and when after the week's build-up the visit was made, a wonderful afternoon took place when the children put air in tyres, crawled under engines and finally worked the pumps. The drawings of the day's events had to be made and Freddy produced a sheet of paper quite bare except for one large spider hanging from a string. This is a typically aphasic reaction. If someone says 'garage' this does not necessarily mean 'car' to the aphasic child. He is enclosed in his own world of limited words and their obscure personalized meanings. He frustrates those living with him because expectations of the obvious reactions to the simplest things are not fulfilled and it is exhausting to have to keep an open mind all the time, even on trivialities. Sometimes we had marvellous surprises and Freddy would hear the word 'picnic' and rush off and get a thermos flask; other times we would try to explain what was going to happen and no words meant anything, in which case we gave up and just took him along till he saw for himself and even then there was no way of fixing in his mind the words relevant to the outing, and so, if it had been a trip to a wildlife park or stately home and was to be repeated, we had to find pictures to try to get him to remember the previous occasion, and if we were successful he would show intense pleasure and go and get the jersey he had worn on the

45

first occasion to show us he remembered it all.

His memory for details like this never ceased to amaze us, but we ached and longed for him to remember and apply words rather than things. Notwithstanding, the projects continued and I believe they paid off since Freddy for one remembers some of the facts about wool and coal today.

'Why' and 'how' were questions asked, never 'where'. The head teacher once told us that she spent half an hour every day for ten days on 'where'. Everybody had got it. The weekend came and went and on Monday morning she started off: 'And now children . . . The faces were all blank and nobody appeared to have ever heard the word 'where'.

If concentrated effort could be measured, the amount expended by those dedicated and devoted people should be registered with the grains of sand in all the seas; ballads should be sung; their names should be in lights. As it is, numbers of boys and girls are now able to take some recognized place in life, who would otherwise have been destined to a most painfully limited and frustrated existence.

Freddy was into his eighth year. Technically things were both good and bad. His vocabulary was steadily increasing. But what was this little boy like? He was easy to live with in that he would spend hours making things out of Lego. His attention to detail was remarkable and again showed his keen observation. As with the fire irons when he was three, he was still relying a lot on his eyes.

We all went to Switzerland to ski after Christmas. As usual, in spite of increased vocabulary, his comprehension was still an enormous hazard and there was still no sense of time. So, as always, he had missed out on all the planning and found himself on a journey one cold morning. He was the best of travellers. Everything was interesting. The train to London and the taxi to Victoria, the journey to Dover, the queuing for passports, detection of luggage, the crush of crowds and finally the steamer, all were a source of tremendous exhilaration for Freddy. Nothing upset him.

While the non-existence of brochure and indeed ticket-scheduled meals reduced Jean to tears and Heather into a state of cemented endurance, Freddy was undismayed and knelt

46

on the green train seats gazing out into the French night hour after hour. It was exciting missing out on baths and thrilling to sleep in clothes. He seemed to find the narrow bunks of the couchette as good as a feather bed and whereas late trains, missed connections and failure of heating systems and carriage lights in temperatures below zero made the rest of us wonder why we ever did this kind of thing, Freddy continued to find everything fascinating and smiled and smiled.

Things were different on arrival. He was dreadful about the food and would have starved had it not been for the bread which he loved and ate prodigiously. He did not really take to skiing and of course he could not understand the instructors. He stood about and his hands and feet got cold. The rest of us were trying to have a holiday and were all bitten by the skiing bug, so Freddy was a real drag on our patience and in the end we hardened our hearts and sent him to his classes in the mornings and took it in turns to sledge with him in the afternoons.

We pressed on relentlessly with ski holidays for two reasons. One was that it was indescribable joy for us, the thing we dreamed of from one winter to the next, and, more important, we knew that sooner or later Freddy would acquire the knack and then share our enthusiasm. The second was that we felt it would give him some confidence, and in time that is just what it did do. After-skiing was a problem. Jean and Heather made friends with other skiers and we were trying to get some reading done but Freddy was disorientated, missed his home surroundings and belongings, and somehow the box of Lego which always went with us seemed to lose most of its magic on the floors of Swiss hotel bedrooms or inadequate tables in noisy bars. He always showed excitement when cases were finally repacked because it meant more hopeful travel again which he certainly found better than arriving.

On his return to school after this first ski expedition he made several drawings. Needless to say they consisted entirely of the journeys and, again, his detailed observation was most marked. In one narrow valley we had all noticed some electricity pylons anchored against the mountainside at a most unusual angle, leaning out over the valley. These came into the drawings along with a bird's eye view into our compartment which contained

47

objects particular to each of us. He knew which girl's suitcase was which and Heather's teddybear which accompanied her everywhere was to be seen in a corner of the carriage, and Jean's knitting, drawn very small.

His teacher reported that he had a lot to say about the ski trip, so perhaps it was just like so many other British activities, wonderful when it stopped. Another interesting thing happened about this time which showed us how much Freddy used his eyes. Some friends came for tea. About eight months previously we had all gone on a picnic together. Freddy came into the drawing room dragging an old tartan rug and he put it on the visitors' knees. We all looked blankly at him and then I remembered the picnic and realized this was Freddy's way of saying how he remembered them from that outing. We made a fuss of him and he understood that we understood, and thus some apparently vital communication-identity-participation need within him was satisfied. We were much encouraged that he wanted to be wholly involved and these incidents made us acutely aware of this problem for him.

It was plain that he was making progress in life but he was painfully young for eight. Although it was easy in that one simply planned his life for him and he happily followed, it was at the same time alarming because of his helplessness over so many things.

If he had got lost, he could not have managed an address. He spoke his name rather indistinctly, but could not write it, and he had no idea of the name of the town where he lived. On car journeys when we were all together we just talked over him.

Sometimes he would look lost and deserted and then one of us would say something which he could cope with and make him feel included.

His grammar and phrasing was unique and illogical. Numerous phrases he used were understood by the family but made no sense to other people. One phrase which took four years to straighten out was 'Have we went going before here we been'. This would be said on a journey, and was sometimes a question, sometimes an answer. It expressed recognition of a route we had previously taken. For the same length of time he mixed up 'he' and 'she' and for much longer, 'breakfast',

48

'lunch', 'tea' and 'dinner' and it was pure chance if he got the right word with the right meal. As for mother, father, sister, brother, son, daughter, uncle, etc., I often wonder if the more extreme ramifications of family relationships will ever be clear in his mind. Sums meant nothing and it began to look as though even the simplest were going to be unteachable. There were so many things it was impossible to explain. On the other hand, he developed a passion for Roman history, and for a very long time pictures of the occupation of Britain by the Romans were the only pictures he wanted to see. One could not put the occupation into any place in time because as with anything that needed explaining, he just did not understand the words used for the explanation and by the time we had stopped and explained them, everybody had forgotten what was being explained in the first place. We all developed double talking habits, those for term-time and those for the holidays. Once the holidays began and Freddy was home we automatically and quite subconsciously only used words we instinctively knew he could manage. Although this was automatic and subconscious, it was the most tremendous strain.

I knew so well what he could and could not understand, that when people met him and began speaking to him and asking him questions I found I either quickly said 'Oh, he wouldn't know that' or automatically translated the questions for him into words I knew he knew. It somehow gave an impression to a lot of people that he was doing fine and understood it all. You just had to live with him to know. When I set myself to try to learn French, it struck me how Freddy and I made the same grammatical mistakes. This at first seemed reasonable but then I found it curious because if you already know one language, it is not surprising to confuse it with another, Freddy was making my mistakes with a language he was learning from nothing. I often wondered if he had dreams and thoughts. He was so desperately short of words.

Every holiday we had a check-up at a hearing clinic. They had no time for aphasia and believed Freddy was exclusively partially deaf and should be at a school catering for this condition. Some of the aphasic specialists were loath to admit to any hearing loss and would have him exclusively aphasic! When he copied words from the board, backwards spelling was creeping in and there were endless gods for dogs and ot's for to's, so it looked as though he was having dyslexia as well. And this condition was rejected by both medical parties. Only the teachers at the John Horniman school were free from prejudice, except for a passionate one in favour of any means at all by which their children might get help and relief.

The school was putting on the Christmas pantomime. The choice was Cinderella and Freddy was one of the sisters. The previous year he had only qualified to be some silent ignominious gnome, so this was promotion indeed. Everybody had a part and everybody managed to say something. Freddy looked magnificently ugly with skeins of blue wool for hair, a satin dress, a lot of make-up and a Victorian lavatory chain hung round his neck complete with porcelain handle. The children were word perfect and the concentration was intense. The school was electrified with important excitement. The whole show had been planned on a positive Mulberry Harbour scale, and shared with that other human endeavour many of the same hazards and also its supreme success. First, anyone other than those particular teachers would have decided it was impossible and would have done something else or nothing at all. Secondly, it required exhaustive planning and research to find a speaking part for twenty-four virtually non-speaking children. Thirdly, the hazards of cues and forgotten and misunderstood lines bristled so sharply that superhuman patience and determination was required for its execution, but against all odds of time and ideas it worked. There are still bits of the Mulberry floating about in the Channel at Arromanches and there are bits of that pantomime that will be floating about in my mind and Freddy's until we both float on.

At the end of the following spring term, when Freddy was going to be nine, the great assessment was to take place.

At the end of the previous summer I had tried Freddy's winter clothes on him. To my consternation and surprise, the pyjamas I had made when he first went off to school still fitted. They were going to wear out long before he required any sleeves or legs let down. I talked to my husband about this, and sure enough, during those three and a half years at school he simply had not grown.

What with the shock of going to school in the first place

50

and then the strain of keeping going and the mental effort required in an unending struggle to be a person with other people, we reckoned that something had had to give, and in Freddy's case it was the growing. It seemed that his body, unable to cope with everything, had dispensed with the least necessary function at that particular time. This did seem logical, nevertheless it was alarming, and the only advantage was the social one of camouflage. He did not look like a boy approaching his ninth year. He looked like a child of six and in consequence, was treated as such. It did help.

Apparently everyone was in on the assessment act, and after all the nine-year-old children's cases had been gone through, from every angle, it was decided by the teachers and speech therapists and doctors of the original school we visited whether these children should move on there or take their chance in normal schools. It was decided that Freddy needed further special schooling, so he was to move to a senior school the next term. It was very sad saying goodbye to this one which had done so much for him, and although we knew he would never lose touch, it was a great wrench for us all. Freddy had been with other children on a coach visit to the next school so it was not going to be too strange. He did not remember being taken there by us at three-and-a-half, but the new school was always being mentioned in various contexts so that the children got the idea that it was where everyone went next.

Of course not everyone did go, and the teachers and speech therapist often talked to us of the feelings they had about the children who were not considered bad enough or 'suitable' to move on. These children had to take pot luck in ordinary state schools and it did not seem possible to us that any of them could hope to cope.

Some time after Freddy's move, the Sembal Trust asked the school speech therapist to do a research project into this situation, and she travelled the country visiting all the children who had been at the John Horniman school and then gone into ordinary education. She told us that in almost every case the results had been disastrous.* The large classes and the complete ignorance of the teachers about aphasia, mild or otherwise, had

* C. P. S. Griffiths, 'A Follow-up Study of Children with Disorder of Speech', *British Journal of Disorders of Communication*, 4, 1969, 46–56.

made mincemeat of these children and she felt that all that had been done for them at their special school had been virtually lost. Many of the children had turned in on themselves in self-defence or from despair. The waste of all the precious effort which we had seen being exerted did not bear contemplation.

Freddy hugged his teachers when he finally said goodbye. They said they were going to miss their founder member but I knew this was nothing to how much he was going to miss them and the wonderful confidence and security which had been established. Before we left with him for the Easter holidays, the matron wished us luck for his future and generously admitted that she had made a mistake with Freddy at the beginning, and that if she had known then all that she had since learnt through living with this kind of child, she would most certainly have let me stay in the hotel and settle him as I had wanted.

The shock, those four years ago, had rendered Freddy punch-drunk at the time, and it had taken all of the first year before there had been any really hopeful signs of response. I was glad that others were to be spared the ordeal we had undergone. It was a pity that ideas had been so fixed and minds so closed.

But he was responding now, and the head teacher said it was his concentration which was winning him the day. He seemed to be someone who really hammered at things, especially when interested. Over the business of arithmetic there was no determination at all, as non-comprehension here seemed to be complete.

4

That holiday we all went to a wedding. Freddy stood on the pew in the church, the better to see the bride come down the aisle, and clapped his hands and said 'Queen'. He happily thought it was HM, no doubt descended from some school picture complete in coronation robe. When would we be able to explain what a constitutional monarch was? How and why. The elementary intellect required for abstract thought and exercises such as $x=0$ he just did not have and, similarly, the symbolic concept of a monarch representing a country was not within his grasp. Later that holiday the girls and Freddy and I set off to Tunis to stay with Tanya. Her husband was a correspondent in North Africa and this was a great adventure as Freddy's travel experiences were to be extended to the air. We left London in grey drizzle and arrived at Tunis airport to see swaying palms against a black and windy sky, but next morning the sun was up and we looked out onto a brilliantly foreign world. I had never forgotten the doctor who said we must make life stimulating and perhaps it was this that spurred us on to expeditions. We were lucky to have an exciting person to stay with in a thrilling country.

Tanya's husband was on business in Algiers and she was on holiday from the school where she taught and devoted the whole week to making life interesting for us. She succeeded. We went for picnics, we saw pots and baskets and brasses being made in primitive villages. We saw camels pulling ploughs and Arabs in striped dressing gowns riding on the tail end of donkeys, all looking as though they had stepped straight out of an illustrated Bible. We wandered through the alleys of a walled city, we swam, we had camel rides and we watched Tanya effectively bargaining in the markets. Flower stalls in the main street of Tunis were one of the most exotic things we had ever seen, riots of lilies, carnations and roses. There were beautiful museums with rescued mosaics and there was Carthage. Freddy was in his element surrounded by Roman pillars, frescoes and urns. We met a number a local inhabitants, French engineers searching for oil, several Tunisian doctors, diplomats from some of the African embassies, students and local families. It was here that Freddy first discovered his taste for champagne. He didn't really need it. His spirits were high as it was, but at the end of a picnic day, when we had all been dancing in a café on the way home and were feeling wild and gay, Tanya remembered there was some champagne in the fridge. She gave Freddy a glass. He drank it straight off, hesitated, looked round and then ran into the drawing room, made a bee-line for the sofa, leapt on to it and turned two somersaults. We put on the latest records and he continued in this vein until bedtime. He danced and did more somersaults, demanded more champagne and lived out a glorious evening of uninhibited gaiety and freedom.

From that time on, his face never failed to light up in a particularly interested way if he heard the magical word 'champagne'. The sun beat down, the palm trees were quite still as we left for home and the new school.

The first two-thirds of our journey to the new school were the same as that taken to the old, and somewhere in Hampshire there was a farmer who went in for black sheep. These had been a source of encouraging interest on outward journeys and of hilarious jokes and songs on the homeward bound. We were now into our fifth year on this route and the black sheep were safely in their field grazing away with black lambs frolicking around them. They earned but a passing comment, an agreed acceptance of traditional form because the old tensions were back—apprehension, fear of the unknown. We arrived. The school was twice the size of the old one and the boys and girls attended it until school-leaving age, which in some cases was extended to eighteen. There were nice grounds and a cub and scout pack. We were hoping there would be some really well organized games, particularly football in winter, because Freddy was a good shape in spite of being small, had reasonable ball-sense and, whereas other boys of his age were getting knocked about in games and having to learn to take some rough stuff, he was being cushioned from all blows.

We felt there was quite a lot to be said for this easy way of

54

life, but it wasn't very realistic. We were taken up to see a small dormitory with tidy beds and a shoe-polishing chest on a landing. One other boy and a girl from the JH school had made the move with Freddy so he had some familiar faces around and with this fact to comfort ourselves, we made the arrangements about pocket money, hearing-aid batteries and outings and left for home. This school was a non-maintained, Ministry-recognized special school for children suffering from speech and language disorders. Freddy did not speak well but was often quite intelligible. He spoke as he heard and he did not hear very well. His problem was primarily one of educability.

There was improvement in his comprehension, but there were still Siberian wastes here and it was impossible to get across to him any abstract ideas. We hoped the new school was going to get him on well with learning. He was nine and quite soon it was going to matter about reading and writing and sums.

He was there for two years and he was not happy. As his speaking improved he was able to give us a picture of long, empty weekends with a cramped common room and very little supervision. It was patently obvious that weekends and particularly Sundays were spent listless and bored. I arrived to take him out one Sunday and was told the children were at church. I crept into the service late, spotted the two rows of children in a side aisle and sat quietly behind them. One child had a dreadful runny nose which no one was doing anything about, and there were several torn raincoats, missing buttons and unravelled jersey sleeve edges. I had a wild longing to install myself in the school and become a Mrs Tiggy-Winkle to them all. The service was long and dreary, with a twenty-minute sermon. Freddy was painfully pleased to see me and we set about filling in the rest of the day as we were too far from Granny's haven to motor over there. For the rest of his time at this school I had to steel myself not to think about him on Sundays. There was nothing one could do and I found Sundays were lasting longer than they used to; when clocks struck eight in the evening, dark clouds lifted and dispersed, wherever I was and whatever I was doing, as I thought of him in bed at last, his day over.

What he was enjoying was his school work and his letters were written free hand and improving. Whether he copied from

55

blackboards or not, we never had 'Dear' spelt the same way twice. He knew the letters D, E, A and R made up this word, but the order in which they went apparently had no meaning whatever and we would get all variations from Dere, Drea, Daer, Drae to an occasional Der. The letters never really told us anything, and as with the spider at the garage, some celebrity could have been in the place but all we would hear about was a good pudding!

Beautifully produced and very elaborately staged plays took place each year but they were so professionally organized and rehearsed that the vital ingredient of total involvement by the children seemed to be missing. Freddy made no great attachments at this place, and except for enthusiasm about the classroom his heart, I felt, was cold.

I spoke to some other parents as we queued to pay for our tea and biscuits after the various end-of-term celebrations. They were all in a state of acute anxiety. Some suffered from anxiety in reverse, from the relief of having their offspring accepted, and were settling for this fact alone and not daring to look outside or beyond it. Some, whose children were nearing leaving age, were numbed to the point of paralysis by the haunting fear of what next.

The school changed to four terms. Everybody welcomed this. Those three terms were very long indeed and experience was showing that the amount of sustained concentration and effort vital from both staff and pupils was proving too great. By the tenth week everyone had reached saturation point. So four shorter terms with those heaven-sent breaks between, were a great improvement and relieved a lot of pressure.

Skiing was working out better. By this time Freddy had got the knack and was really enjoying it. Hotel life was still a bore and so was food, but all this was worth the one great fact that here was something Freddy was doing that not everyone could do, and what was more he was actually doing it better than some people. One of the best things about skiing is that though nearly everyone is better than you, you are bound to be better than *someone* else, and at all levels it is fun.

Camping in the summer had turned from rain to sun, as we were now on the west coast of France. More travel and sand and sea, practically no clothes and an echo of Tunisia. Very, very happy days. At 4 pm a large lady appeared on our beach with a vast box slung round her shoulders containing roasted peanuts, chocalate and ice cream. She came calling 'Cacaou-ettes, chocolats, glaces' in a sing-song voice and Freddy caught onto this and it became a phrase in the family which we all sang out whenever ice creams were bought in France or at home. The girls made friends with French children on the beach and in the field where we camped and they happily included Freddy in their games and no-one noticed his problem as it was generally accepted that one so small would know no foreign languages. One year a happy young carpenter gave him rides on his motor-cycle early each morning as he chugged off to buy the bread, and Freddy took an interest in any marketing expedition, becoming fascinated by frogs for sale ready dressed and pinned out on boards. He liked the sacks of spices, the handsome old ladies in long black dresses with silver hair shining beneath black crocheted nets and the way they stood in booths offering fowls and herbs from their small-holdings and back-yards.

At home, our regular visits to the hearing clinic continued and our GP and the ENT specialist were still kind and interested in Freddy's progress.

Freddy was going to be eleven years old, and his destiny was about to be partially sealed. It is a very, very good thing that we never know what is going to happen. Out of the blue we were informed by post that he was fit for normal education and should leave at the end of the early summer term. We made plans to go to the school to talk, as Freddy's reading age had been assessed as that of a child of six, his writing was barely intelligible and letters we had written saying this had produced no replies.

When we arrived we were shown into a room with a large dining table and chairs and no one suggested we sat down. The principal came in and we prepared to ask our questions about Freddy's future. She stated loud and clear that his speech had improved so much while at the school that he was quite ready for normal schooling. His speech in fact was not good, even if it was a lot better than that of some of the other children. We pointed out that he could not do sums, still could not read, could barely write and still had a gross comprehension problem. In view of all this, what school did she know of that would take him? She said she was quite sure that there were many private preparatory schools who would be happy to have him. My husband pointed out that the function of preparatory schools was to prepare boys for the common entrance or the 11 plus examination to qualify them for public or grammar schools, and that boys of Freddy's present age attending these schools had already been learning French and Latin for at least three years, not to mention geometry, algebra and general science. There was a pause, a flurry and then a repetition of the statement that he was fit for normal education.

It was like being told 'He seems bright enough to me' all over again and I asked the principal how she thought he would get on in a secondary school in a large class, unable to read. My question was ignored. Finally when tension had mounted to an electric pitch and I was holding fast to my handbag, we asked her how the phrase 'ready for normal education' could possibly be applied to a child of eleven who could not read or write. Why couldn't he stay longer where he was as lessons were going so well? The principal suddenly left the room leaving the door wide open and we both thought she had gone to fetch a file or one of the teachers. We waited. We waited longer. We waited longer still, and then it slowly dawned upon us that, unbelievably, we had had our answer.

It felt peculiar as we walked slowly out of this house full of people which was suddenly empty and silent. Not a soul or the sound of one in the hall. No distant chink of kitchen noise or faint classroom rumble. No gardener outside, no face at any window. It was like a sinister film without background music and the car doors seemed to echo in the midday sunshine as we slammed them shut and crunched our way round the rosebeds and set off for home. We were utterly bewildered and could not take in what had happened. It all felt so unreal that we acted as though we had had a violent dream, the effects of which were going to wear off when we became fully conscious. But we had not been asleep and the effects remained and hung over our day. We recalled the event in every detail again and again to make quite certain that the principal really had walked out on us rather than answer our questions, and it was so. The effects returned on waking next day.

There was that depressing sensation of emerging from sleep,

becoming conscious and instantly feeling oppressed. 'What was wrong?' I asked myself, and then all the events of the previous day crowded back into my mind in a nightmare of remembering. I lay in bed going over it all again and then turned to reasoning with myself and telling myself that it had all been a mistake and that there would be a letter of explanation. Of course! That was it. There had simply been a mistake and if there wasn't a letter already waiting downstairs, then one would come with the second post or at latest next day.

No letter ever came. In that ten-minute interview with the principal our lives had been changed. When she walked out of that room, she took with her the last vestige of security we were ever to know, and after that I discovered what it was like to wake up every day and be filled with fear.

We sent a letter asking for help and advice and repeating our hopes that Freddy might be allowed to stay on one more year in view of his general backwardness. Our letter was ignored, or at least never answered, and we wrote to the doctor who had originally diagnosed the aphasic condition but he was away and had by this time retired anyway. It then transpired that the report on Freddy had been sent with his whole history to our local education officer.

Freddy's reaction when he was told he could not stay at this school any longer was mixed. He was instantly full of hope that the next one would be better. He said 'No more Sundays' but hastily added the names of three teachers whom he had liked, particularly a Mrs D. During the ensuing holiday he found a brown moth which he felt was special and took a lot of trouble finding some cotton wool, organizing it into a match-box and asking me to wrap it up and post it.

I helped him to write a letter saying who it was from, and in time it got posted off to Mrs D. From the moment it disappeared across the post office counter he anticipated Mrs D's reply. We explained about the time it would take to reach her and then that maybe she was away on holiday. I forget now if he ever heard from her. I believe he did, but the letter came so long after the event that it was almost meaningless. At the time the moth was sent off, her letter would have meant so much and its not coming just added to the general depression we were feeling at the time. It left Freddy feeling irrevocably cut off from the place where he had spent two years; he was a person who thrived on having ties. Gathering no moss was contrary to his nature and, in spite of not much enjoying the school, he would have appreciated some link with the place. We had a lasting link with the John Horniman school and Freddy continued to call in there for years.

5

When we telephoned our Local Authority Education Office to see what they thought about things, they expressed concern and said we would hear from them. We then went to the Child Guidance Clinic where we met the consultant psychiatrist. He was one of the kindest, most helpful people and became deeply interested in Freddy and his history and, more important, his future. He stressed that the potential he had was good and *must* be reached at all costs. He was tremendously pleased that Freddy was well-adjusted and emotionally balanced, he saluted him on this account and commended him as having guts. Freddy felt saluted and glowed and expanded in the presence of this encouraging person. We made several visits to him and Freddy underwent tests with him and he talked to us a lot and finally made a recommendation that Freddy should go to a special school nine miles away, run by an outstanding woman who had children suffering from various defects. He arranged for us to go and see her and in due course the day arrived.

It was perfect. A large house set in good grounds, a swimming pool and, best of all, old stables converted into an art block and run by a young sculptor with quiet ways and a fund of exciting ideas, all relative to the children's problems. He was wandering about the grounds with five of them and they were picking up things and he was teaching them to notice—old match-boxes, bits of sheep's wool, nails and paper—all used for constructing shapes and making patterns.

He had some potting in process and a boy with muscular dystrophy in a wheelchair was making mosaics on a tray on his knees. All was voluntary silence and calm, springing from intense absorption and involvement. It was a question of *dragging* Freddy away. The headmistress explained how every one assembled in the hall each morning to the strains of classical music which she had relayed in the passages. She said she felt so little was generally heard these days and that it was nice for the children to get used to the strains of Bach and Mozart, and her aim was that it should all become part of their lives and be taken for granted as much as pop. Her children were chronic asthmatics, spastics, were deeply emotionally disturbed, had weak hearts, and other troubles. One child who was physically perfect but upset brain-wise was helping another who was very bright but had his legs in calipers. The school seemed to be one very large family where everyone was accepted and where they learnt to accept.

Freddy felt at home at once, and there were sixty children which was good as it was larger than the last school and this meant wider experiences. A taxi was organized to collect and deliver the children from our town who attended the school. Freddy would be making their number up to five. There were no boarders, and we could not believe our luck. There was apparently a desperate shortage of places but Freddy had been called to see the MOH of this town and after he had given him a Beatrix Potter book to read and had been carefully through the consultant psychiatrist's report, he decided that as Freddy had got so far, it was essential to keep the good work going. He put his name forward as a priority and Freddy was accepted for the next term.

The people at the Hearing Clinic were still advocating schools for the partially deaf, but we always felt they would be too limited and that he might not get enough attention paid to the non-comprehension side of his problem.

Years ago when his hearing loss had first been recognized, Freddy had taught himself to lip-read and with that and the hearing aid and the hope of a new one with a battery at the back of the ear which would put an end to the delicate flex which got in the way all the time, we felt he was better with the broader schooling.

We had been to see a Rudolph Steiner school who were keen to have him and confident that they could help, but every other child there was severely physically handicapped and we did feel that it was becoming vital that Freddy got some organized games and a chance to knock about. We had mentioned Rudolph Steiner to our Education Officer during one conversation but he made a passing comment that he never sent children to 'those places'. There is still a prejudice against the Rudolph Steiner schools and one really wonders why when the proof of their enormous successes is there for all the world to see. Does the world want to?

Games at this school consisted of swimming and gymnastics, but it was a day school and we were confident that we could get football organized from home on Saturdays. Everything seemed to be ideal and we were very happy about it.

The term began on 5 September and when we returned from camping, towards the end of August, I was dismayed to find no brown envelope containing instructions about the taxi.

To dispel my now intuitive distrust of any arrangements in the hands of officialdom, I told myself that people were on holiday. I told myself this but I did not believe it, and yet I had to because I could not admit the awful thought that at the last minute Freddy might be prevented from going to the school.

We went to Yorkshire for an 'end of holidays' treat', but the time spent there was haunted by that envelope and as we reached home again I was stepping out of the car before it had stopped and fumbling with the key and plunging into the pile of letters waiting for us.

It was not there and it was 1 September. On 4 September we telephoned the school and the headmistress apologized profusely and asked us if we could possibly do the transport ourselves while she looked into the matter as she could not understand what had happened or not happened.

I took Freddy to the school armed with the inevitable shoe bag containing his gym shoes and a comb, and a small boy was waiting to be his guide. Every new pupil had a guide provided for his or her first week. I collected Freddy at the end of the day and hoped to see someone with taxi news but there was no one about and I did not want to be a nuisance on such a busy day, so we left it and prepared to take him again in the morning. He had had a marvellous day and spent the afternoon in the Art block. At the end of the second day I called in at the school office where I was greeted by a distracted headmistress. She had telephoned our Education Office to enquire about the taxi and had met with anger and abuse. Freddy, they said, had no right whatever to be at her school. The consultant's recom-

63

mendation had not been approved, there was no question of reversing this decision and that was all they had to say.

This very beautiful lady and I looked at each other in deep silence. She knew she could help Freddy and I knew she could. What did it all mean? If the education officer was not going to pay, could we pay for him ourselves? No, it was a school run by the city fathers and only received children on the recommendation of Local Authorities. What had gone wrong? And why? Freddy was still muddled about time and though one could not talk in terms of years, he now understood 'tomorrow' and as I drove him home I could not bring myself to tell him it was 'no go' next day. The headmistress said she was sorely tempted to let him continue attending while she put in a plea but felt it would be less jeopardizing if she complied with the education officer's wishes while her plea was in process.

After bath time and when I had finished reading to Freddy —a routine we tried to keep to regularly—I faced the music and told him the news.

He turned very red and then he cried. They were tears of bewilderment and intense disappointment. He felt betrayed and I felt like his betrayer. He had a clay model half finished and wanted it and what was more, he wanted to make another. The gloom was leaden and we all went to bed that night feeling desolate and when I went up to kiss Jean and Heather I found them both in tears too.

Next morning my husband took some time off to telephone the Education Office. After ten minutes' wait he was put through to the education officer himself. They spoke for three-quarters-of-an-hour at the end of which an appointment was reluctantly given for a personal interview. The talk on the telephone consisted of my husband trying to find out why permission to attend this school was being withheld and the education officer saying that special education for Freddy was no longer necessary. When I heard that he was going to see the officer in person the following week, I relaxed because I knew that a good discussion of the whole situation would sort everything out. I did say to my husband that it was time the officer saw and spoke to Freddy himself and that then all would become clear to him. He agreed and said this was going to be his main request when the time came. The days slid slowly by

64

and at last it was time. We were welcoming some new staff to our school that night and I was arranging some flowers when my husband left the house. I knew he would not be long because government officials always see as little of potential complainers as possible. Time passed. One hour, another half. What was happening? I knew it was merely a matter of form. They couldn't not understand about Freddy, they had the report and recommendation from the Child Guidance Clinic; perhaps they felt they had spent money enough on him already but if they stopped now it would undo all they had done. They couldn't stop now, he couldn't cope in an ordinary school, he couldn't, he just couldn't.

I heard the distinctive click of our front door and my husband was in the room. His face was pale grey and covered with tiny lines. He said: 'I saw the education officer and MOH and I've been begging them for one-and-a-quarter hours to see the child for themselves and they refuse. They say there is no need as they have it all on paper and it says there that he is now fit for normal education. I pointed out that whatever the paper says the fact remains that he is not sub-normal but he cannot read or write and that this is not normal. They both stood stolidly waving a bundle of papers and repeatedly quoting this phrase, "fit for normal education". I asked them if they always went on reports and never actually saw the people concerned and what about the report from the Child Guidance Clinic. They wouldn't reply directly. I mentioned the two days Freddy had had at that school and how successful they had been and did they not think this disruption a fairly damaging thing to do to a child, particularly one in as sensitive a situation as this. Again, no direct answer. The education officer said there is a place for him at our local secondary school and that is where he ought to be and he can start next Monday. There is a limit to how long you can survive, hitting your head against a brick wall, so I came away. They absolutely will not see Freddy though I did tell them that three minutes' conversation with him would reveal all to them.'

It wasn't a sinking feeling so much as a sensation of everything draining away. I was standing by the mantelpiece and I clutched the grey marble while everything turned cold and I felt my legs giving way under me.

The most alarming thing of all was that I already knew about this, and knew very well; thoughts as sharp as needles were sparklering through my head, thoughts about power and people's destinies in the hands of other people. My head vibrated with all the nightmares I had ever had: the consciousness of the eighth of me which is Jewish being enough to have sent us to concentration camps had we lived in Germany in the 1930s; being shot down and trapped by flames in a bomber during the war; sinking in a submarine or caught by a direct hit in a tank; the tortures suffered by those who fell into Japanese hands; and then, later, nightmares about the children being kidnapped or something happening to my husband; the terror of being unemployed which influenced my life after reading *Love on the Dole*. All these real, unreal fantasies flew through my mind and crystallized themselves into the one thing I had never dreamt about which was the stark shattering reality of Kafka revealed IN MY LIFE. I had read and thought I understood Kafka from the security of my armchair as I had read Orwell's *1984*, but now it was actually happening and I saw all too plainly that here could madness lie. Everything Shakespeare and Tolstoy had shown me was so:

Circumstances may alter. People never.

And how were we to cope with those circumstances which were undermining our morale with every 'hour minute' that passed? Like K, we were trapped in a corridor whose doors when we thankfully reached them melted away into nothingness and Freddy was alive and determined to go on living but this place was nowhere. 'For God's sake,' I told myself, 'this is Britain.'

And we were Britons, but we did not feel at all free. We felt like galley slaves battened down and coming hard against a gigantic enemy, unseen but hugely threatening, wielding unlimited and apparently unquestioned power.

I remembered that we had guests coming, people we didn't know and in ten minutes' time. Like automata we went through the motions of entertaining. Our guests were young, had just undertaken a responsible job and were in the first flush of success at having got it, enthusiastic and full of splendid ideas about it. They left at 11 pm and then we got down to our thinking. What to do? Who to ask? How did it all work? We

66

decided for the sake of peace to send Freddy to the secondary school where, if nothing else, he would have some company and certainly the wretched football we had been clamouring for. This while we thought and planned.

Two days later I answered the telephone and our education officer announced himself. In honeyed tones he said he had contacted the headmaster of the junior school housed under the same roof as the secondary school and had asked him whether he was prepared to make an exception of Freddy and take him into his class of eight-year-olds and that the head-master had graciously agreed to this which he, the education officer, thought so nice of him. I was so dumbfounded I could not get any words out at all. 'Are you there?' called the voice, a trifle less honeyed. 'Yes' I replied. 'Well then,' he said, 'the headmaster will be expecting the boy on Monday.' I thanked him and replaced the receiver. Did he consider this normal education? Why this ridiculous contravening of laws here and not in the case of the other school? An eleven-and-a-half-year-old secondary school child in a junior school class of eight-year-olds indeed! That he could stand there dominating my husband, bulldozing him into a state of impotent resignation, only to contradict everything as soon as his back was turned! In total bewilderment and a deal of fear, I waited for my husband to come in.

What a pity, I thought, that the head of the junior school had agreed to take Freddy. What would have happened if he had refused? I wondered. But of course the education officer is his employer, isn't he? And one usually complies with the boss's wishes if one wants to keep one's job and get on.

The more I thought about the education officer's arrangements the more scandalous they seemed. I telephoned the consultant of the Child Guidance Clinic and told him what had happened. He too was completely baffled and said he thought it sounded extremely unsatisfactory. I begged him to speak again for Freddy, but he explained that he existed in a purely advisory capacity and had no authority by which to dictate. He added that this was the first time advice given by him to the Education Authority had not been taken up and acted on. I asked him if he had any idea why. He replied that he had none but that we must remember that everyone was human and that humans cannot always be relied upon to act or think logically. He added as a reminder that we had our Education Committee. We were beginning to learn the forms and we wrote a report and took it to the chairman of the Education Committee with a request that Freddy's case should be reconsidered for a place at the 'two day' school.

What arguments the education officer put up when this came to be considered, we shall never know, but we heard no more. It came to our notice that there was absurd and serious jealousy between towns and boroughs over what they each had and had not in the way of amenities. This town was jealous of that one's open air swimming pool and that one of another's new comprehensive or art school. We were incredulous, but as time went on and we had more dealings with local bureaucracy we very reluctantly came to believe that it was a real possibility that out of nothing more or less than spite and hurt pride, our town would withhold cooperation with the available amenities of another, even at the expense of the well-being and possible whole future of a person.

Education officers are answerable only to the Minister of Education himself. I had lived my life in total ignorance and absolute unawareness that responsibility on this scale was scattered so lightly around the country. My understanding of Tolstoy was very much deepened at this time and I became acutely aware of, and developed a huge sympathy with, his strivings to convince the world that the most evil thing about us and the cause of all our worldly ills is the domination of people by people. Tolstoy failed to provide a workable alternative. He left behind a marvellous idea as impractical as Christianity literally carried out and I had to remind myself that this same bureaucracy had smilingly, and without a word, made itself responsible for Freddy's attendance at his first splendid school, thus proving that very often and perhaps most of the time it worked well. But it wasn't working now and somehow when it doesn't work, it is extra bad.

While all this was happening, someone who knew about Freddy but did not know what was going on at the time asked me to join a committee being formed to help spastic children in a school which was to be started in the town. My instant reaction was to refuse and I remember being shocked to be

68

asked as I did not believe those children could benefit from amateurs. Just because we had Freddy and his problems, it had not turned me into a professional or someone who understood how to cope any better than anyone else, and I also remember thinking that it would be nice to have time to think and know about other children in like predicaments but that until we had got Freddy off the ground, I had nothing to offer. I made time to be interested in boys' clubs and literary festivals, and a life-saving distraction they were, but anything to do with defective children only made me want to run away. We had our own and he was proving too much for us so I closed my eyes tight to all others, and I remember saying to someone who recounted the sad predicament concerning a mentally defective child, 'Don't tell me, I can't bear it and I don't want to know.' My own house was in terrible disorder and until it was put straight I had nothing to say to anyone.

6

I was plunged into such depths of despairing unbelief that I felt I must somehow be wrong about everything. It seemed to me that if our education officer could act as he had, then he and others like him could do anything, and one had to take it only a step or two further and we would all be in Siberia. In order to try to get myself feeling sane about everything I took our problem to the head of a nearby educational establishment. This man and his wife both held positions of responsibility in public and I felt that they, being professionals, would probably have the answer to what we should do next. Their reaction was a shattering surprise. They were infinitely kind and patiently heard me out, but when it came to the bit about the education officer insisting that Freddy was normal and then making an elaborate exception of him in the junior school, they seemed reluctant to believe, asked if I was quite sure of my facts and then said they could think of nothing anyone could do. They were very sympathetic but I was mad for action and cycled away regretting that I had taken up their time.

I also burdened some kind friends of ours with myself and my quite uncontrollable emotions about this injustice. It was a Saturday when Freddy and I cycled nine miles to see them. We both needed the distraction of physical exertion. The girls were coming home from school every day to a household charged with tension. I apologized to them for my distraction and they seemed to understand that this particular Saturday was important to me. 'Don't worry, Mum,' Jean said, 'We'll give Dad tea when we come in from games' and they flew out of the house with their hockey sticks and fiddle cases and the last night's homework.

Our friends' house was old and stony. Sun-kissed and solid. Spindleberry trees grew wild in the garden which was a tangle of lavender, tobacco plant and Redouté roses. If one stayed there, one's sleep was like the thickness of the walls and the flagged floor in the kitchen, the oak settle and Welsh dresser in the hall reflected quality and rich wisdom, but none of these things compared with the effect and impact of the reality of themselves.

They were generous in a rare way, in that they would interrupt their own lives, stop and make dishes of tea, give time to listen, think terribly carefully, talk, go on thinking long after one had left and make tedious phone calls or spend time writing on one's behalf after further contemplation. There were two boys in their household. One, David, was Freddy's age, artistic, sensitive and extraordinarily project-minded. There was always some colossal undertaking in hand. The younger, Ted, was an indispensable mate to the elder. A hander of vital hammers, a fixer of crucial wheels.

The end of summer still hung around in the air and old hay smells wafted about our heads. Heavy summer green hung on the trees and when we arrived, we all went up the steep hill at the back of the house to fly the rather good aeroplane-kite contraptions we had brought home from our French camping. They had been all the rage in France that year and they made a marvellous engine clatter-whirr as one got them flying into the wind. There was a good breeze that afternoon and the boys soon had their machines moaning and whirring away and were playing the long nylon strings and trying to loop loops.

But Freddy's developed plastic fatigue and the string got knotted and nothing we did could make it fly. He was still suffering acutely from not being allowed to attend the 'two day' school and the collapse of his aeroplane-kite was just about the last straw, a symbol and a sickening reminder of the plunging landslide our lives had become. I lay on the sheep-nibbled turf smelling the thyme and gazing deeply into the heart of a brilliant bacon-and-egg flower and there seemed to be just no rhyme, reason or hope. My friend knew what was going on and she set about finding the trouble with Freddy's synthetic remains. But even she with all her ingenuity could not get it to fly and in the end we stumbled our way homewards. She said she had no words of comfort or encouragement to offer on the bureaucratic front, and that we were in for an endless, exhausting and depressing struggle if we were going to continue to argue with authority, but she also said that they believed Freddy to have a huge potential and the kind of spirit which they felt would 'out' whatever. She was aware that this was thin comfort for us at that particular moment, but the way she said it injected me with renewed determination though as this coursed through my veins like alcohol I still quailed, feeling inadequate, ill-armed and helpless. Yet these feelings had to be squashed because one could not stand in front of this person, look into those eyes and give up; nor could we let Freddy down; so we were going to have to go on, and as Freddy and I set off on our bikes for home, the feelings of inadequacy were still there and were depressing but dying embers of hope were beginning to flicker faintly.

Freddy did not know how lucky he was with the growing army of friends and their marvellous moral support adding strength to our battle.

As a final effort before subjecting him to the wasteland, we wrote to Millfield. This was a school run by a very individual-minded man who had fixed ideas on some rather good things and the most openly wide mind on education. We explained our predicament and we cried for help. He took the trouble to answer by return, a letter written in his own hand.

He hated turning anyone away, he said, particularly some-one with a handicap, but as they had never had anyone in the school suffering from hearing loss and consequently had no specially trained staff, he did not feel the child could gain any-thing worthwhile from being there. Fair enough, it had been worth trying.

So Freddy was armed with a navy blue blazer, the old shoe bag with the gym shoes and a rather ugly cap, and together we cycled through the autumn leaves, scattering chestnuts as our wheels spun over the sticky dampness of the black roads.

He sat in the front row in a class of forty-four eight-year-olds and was taught every lesson by one woman. She could hardly be expected to understand the problems of the partially deaf and whenever she turned her back to write on the blackboard, all her words were lost and lip-reading was of course impossible. He came home with a small book in which there were words whose spellings had to be learnt. We first had to go through a process of trying to explain what the words meant and then

72

tackle the spellings. He got endless rows from his teacher for bad spelling in the tests she gave and the one instance which really clarified the situation was 'butcher' which Freddy spelt 'uch' as that was all he heard of the word. It was good pure spelling to him, but hardly to her and she did not appreciate this and had no time to make exceptions, and possibly no inclination.

He sat through meaningless classes of French, failed to understand any sums, suffered agonies of embarrassment when his turn came for reading aloud and got hopelessly muddled in English and History because so many words sounded alike and became confused. Sheep, sheets, queen, green, scream, scene, bean, preen, dream, geese, etc. all sounded the same and only words of which he really knew the meaning, or knew about from constant usage, swam clearly into his mind. We could only hope and pray that when he learnt to read and gathered more words from the experience of living, the meanings would naturally resolve themselves. He developed aggressive tendencies, fighting for survival in the school-yard in breaks, of which there seemed to be four each day, and only played football once a week. A teacher of the deaf gave him half-an-hour each week when she called at the school and there was no speech therapy. From half-term onwards all work virtually ceased while rehearsals for an elaborate Christmas play began. Freddy's part was that of a silent black slave who came on for one brief moment carrying a cushion—we couldn't say with any confidence that the term had been a success.

We had a young friend waiting for the arrival of a baby to adopt. She was a lively and enthusiastic teacher and agreed to take Freddy for an hour each day after school. So the following term began in earnest and Freddy went straight from school to more school. Shirley had a pretty, neat home with tea waiting each day and she also had a lot of determination. She set about Freddy with an open mind and was very soon completely baffled. But she soldiered on and never ceased trying to think up ways to get round, to by-pass, to get *through*. Freddy moaned and complained about this extra school. He developed a respect for Shirley but found her too much like hard work. It was the only time in the day when consistent concentration was demanded and got, and she was our life-line.

Freddy and I read alternate sentences from adventure books before bedtime, but progress through the books was very slow. With Masefield's *Box of Delights,* every tenth word had to be explained and verb tenses analysed. When it was my turn to read I often cheated and read whole pages very fast, pretending they were one long sentence. It was our only hope of keeping things going and Freddy was totally captivated by the story. When we finally reached the end and it was all revealed as having been a dream, he laughed delightedly with surprise. He had no idea that this was how the fantasy would be resolved, and he was terribly excited because it legitimized the desire he had harboured all along, to believe in it.

But too soon for us Shirley's baby arrived, and that was the end of school after school. We were back to the easy life, there was no pressure and a deadening disinterest and disinclination was jelling alarmingly in Freddy's attitude.

Sometimes I would meet somebody, often a total stranger, and give way to a powerful impulse to tell them about Freddy. I always felt ashamed of the torrent which came pouring out, but it didn't happen very often and always intuitively when it did and in every case something useful came of it. So I found myself on the edge of a hockey-pitch recounting Freddy's history to a man I had never spoken to before. My companion asked if I knew the local teachers' training college held a class on Wednesday mornings for non-reading children from the town. I did not know and could not wait to get things organized. First I saw the man in charge of the class and he explained how the students took the children, under his supervision, and that it was always helpful and useful for them and sometimes beneficial for the children. I then spoke with Freddy's headmaster and asked permission for absence on Wednesday mornings. His attitude was one of complete indifference and in a rather patronizing tone he said I could send the child there if I wanted.

As he was supposed to be well acquainted with Freddy's circumstances and knew of his disabilities I felt he might, if not should, have told me of this service himself. He knew all about it so he certainly could have. I did not believe Freddy was his only pupil with reading problems. Unless the other parents met my friend, how were they going to discover this opportunity?

That first Wednesday, Freddy and I cycled off in a different direction through the maze of the traffic in the centre of the town, noted the one-way streets and found the training college and a bicycle shed.

These Wednesdays became fun, and Freddy revelled in not going to the school. It also meant lunch at home that day and somehow it made the weeks pass more quickly. We never could discover how much actual intellectual aid or enlightenment was given or received. The man in charge of it all was elusive and vague, but Freddy enjoyed going and I was eager for anybody entering the teaching profession to find out how odd his condition was in the hope that they would recognize it in any children they might teach in the future and call it to the notice of their authorities. I also hoped Freddy was with cheerful, open-minded young men in this break from his one-woman-band but it was quite impossible to get an accurate description from Freddy.

One day he asked if friends from school could come to play. I waited with interest to meet them. One was the son of one of the town's clergymen, a big friendly boy with a nice smile who wasn't very brave. One was a French boy, whose father was working at a British factory and had his whole family in England. He had both nerve and charm and a particular kind of fluid grace. The third was short, thickset and very tough, quite impossible to manage and always eating sweets. I felt they were a splendidly-balanced gang. The noise when they were all together was more than a threat to the good relations we had with our neighbours, and I rationed collective visits to two a week.

Freddy was developing some rough habits and while these did no real harm they got him into trouble and demonstrated clearly that aphasia, though lessened to such a great extent, still lurked.

One Wednesday morning he got hold of the newspaper and began looking at the pictures and then found he was late. He did a thing he had never done before. He rushed out of the house without saying goodbye and what was more, he went to school instead of the training college. I was aware of his absence by the strange silence children leave behind and was annoyed with myself for letting him go without reminding him it was

75

Wednesday morning. When he came home at tea-time he got two pieces of my mind, one for not saying goodbye and one for not going to special reading.

The worst punishment one could possibly give Freddy was making him write, and after a glum tea he was sent upstairs to write a letter of apology to the reading-class man for failing to turn up. A furious boy, scarlet with rage, stumped up the stairs. There was silence for a long time. Then I relented and went to help. The letter read thus: 'Dear Mr T, I am sore I ruched out of the house and not sed goodby today.'

It was typically aphasic to miss out on the related significant point and I remembered the spider at the garage. Freddy and I called a truce and after I had explained that Mr T didn't care how he left the house but was interested in him arriving, we sat down and wrote another letter together. I kept the first one and took it to the training college to show them this perfect example of aphasic thinking. I was rather excited about it as I found it fascinating and thought it could be helpful to the students. Alas, I met with complete indifference and, worse, disinterest. In a state of great frustration I cycled hopelessly home. I wanted the whole world to understand about this, but it seemed that nobody wanted to know.

Freddy's speaking was very poor. Some people understood him some of the time, some could not make head or tail of his poor articulation and bad grammar. Our faithful daily, Mrs Cornock, who had heard him growing up, nearly always made successful guesses when she failed to understand various weirdly pronounced or half-said words. But others looked at him with surprise and curiosity. We were becoming alarmed at his non-progress here and could see very clearly that while he was a rather small schoolboy he could get by, but that it was building up to a potentially embarrassing (for him) situation for the future.

We found a friend called Dorothy. She was a recently re-married war widow who had been trained as a speech therapist and had practised almost continuously ever since. She arranged to come once a week after her regular school work. She hammered away at Freddy and, once again, some concentration —sustained concentration—was demanded from him. As with Shirley, this was resented and resisted but out of it all came respect and affection for Dorothy who never gave up and kept enthusiasm and encouragement going in the face of all her own problems of moving house and coping with staff shortages at her ESN school. Here was the splendid professionalism we had encountered at the first school—the great and vital 'give', the one essential for imparting knowledge that seemed to be so rare.

Freddy began to speak better if bullied, and we took over from where Dorothy left off and stepped up our correcting and explaining and insisting. Very often we all just spoke rapidly over his head as there were moments when our lives just had to get a move on and talking went so slowly when including him; but he was becoming more and more aware that a whole exciting life was going on parallel with his own and he was beginning very much to want to participate.

Once a month an orchestra came to our town and I rarely missed their performances. Freddy became infected by my concert anticipation and got it into his head that here was something not to be missed. One week, as the conversation became musical, he announced his desire and indeed intention of coming with me to the 'tonter'. The whole family was going, so tickets were booked and we all set off to the Town Hall. Freddy had gone quite berserk with excitement and insisted on having a bath and sporting a bright red tie and even discarded a pair of shorts as not being clean enough. I felt certain he was in for disappointment, as it was impossible to describe clearly just what a concert consisted of, and no use anyway since he was determined to come with us and that was that. We sat in the gallery and looked down on the stage as the orchestra began to assemble. He enjoyed the look of the double basses and kettle drums, and all was well until the second piece which was for solo violin. Freddy sat next to me with his hands held tight over his ears. The poignant sounds of the violin were about as bad as our Hoover. When I remonstrated with him and eventually got him to remove his hearing aid, he then felt he was missing something, so one could not really win.

At half-time, we queued for squash and suggested some of us went home, but Freddy would have nothing of it and stalwartly sat the entire 'tonter' through.

Nothing more was said about 'tonters' but we did give Freddy

77

a book of Hoffnung cartoons which provided him with unfailing sources of mirth and which he still enjoys. The next thing he latched onto was Stratford. A visit to Mecca, as Stratford is for me, became an insistent 'must' for him. The girls were irritated and impatient when I told them I was going to let Freddy come with us. 'O Mum, *really*,' said Jean, 'he'll never last out and he'll wriggle. We only just make it ourselves, I think it's ridiculous.' 'It's so long' wailed Heather, 'and he'll get so *bored*. He's getting so excited and it's going to be disappointing for him.'

I knew all this *and* that he could not appreciate the play, but we wanted him to have the extending experience of Stratford and as our set policy was to include him in our way of life as much as possible then why not this? And besides, it was Freddy himself who was insisting on coming and I knew he must find out things for himself.

Unfortunately the only tickets we could get at a suitable time and a possible price were for *Love's Labour's Lost*. It was impossible to précis for Freddy this non-plotted play, but no amount of warning that there would be no fights would deter him. I had hoped that the atmosphere would be enough for a start. It was. He sat with shining eyes, gazing at Sally Jacobs' set. The floor of the stage was entirely rush matting and a thrilling light filtered through leafy trees. John Barton made much of the romance. It was light, it was love, but it was also long and as it laboured, I reckoned this time Freddy really wouldn't be able to stay the course, especially as he was given no option of returning home at the interval. Again, we queued for squash and he very nearly wavered, but just managed a brave face and a stiff upper lip. Virtue was certainly rewarded, for when the blissful nonsense ended with the warning from learned men to beware the cuckoo when the meadows are filled with delight, and to be merry like the note of the owl when blood be nipped and ways be foul, two enormous, beautifully made figures, a cuckoo and an owl, were carried on to the stage. The beak of the cuckoo opened in rhythm with the words and a string was pulled to produce 'cuckoo', and the owl had large grey eyelids which clicked slowly over his eyes in appropriate rhythm with *his* words. Freddy was enchanted, and after that he thoroughly understood our enthusiasm for visits to Stratford.

7

His friends continued to call and rag about in the garden and climb trees if it was fine or play with Lego and roar up and down the stairs if wet. If they thought up games with rules like cops and robbers, Freddy became completely overwhelmed. It seemed impossible to explain the rules and he could not grasp what was happening and was accused of spoiling things and then impatience set in, followed by boredom and finally ungracious evacuation. At these times, Freddy got very depressed and looked dejected and forlorn, but after a week or so the friends would begin to trickle back into his life and the not very satisfactory and rowdy relationship would continue in sporadic fits and starts. He needed friends but found it very difficult to adjust to their company. The general talk was of the names of characters from comics, telly shows, football teams; objects discussed were makes of cars, films that had been seen, and spacecraft. All this was over Freddy's head. He never read comics except for *Tin-Tin* books whose pictures he loved and devoured in large quantities. He rarely watched the old telly we had bought and installed in the nursery where the girls watched the Olympic skating and ski-jumping but not much else. As names of friends and acquaintances were still a problem for Freddy, those of footballers and their teams had no significance for him at all.

A car was a car to him and different makes were as nothing; and when he was in a car with us, the various parts such as accelerator and clutch were much too detailed and advanced for him to comprehend and most of the actual words for these parts were too difficult to pronounce. He did, however, go quite mad about the Tiger who appeared at that time and had to be put in our tank. I once drove on an empty tank past three garages for twenty-two miles before we spotted a Tiger when he then allowed me to stop and fill up!

There were very few films he could enjoy as the movement

was so rapid and the plots were too involved to explain to him. As for space, I think he thought it was all to do with bombs in reverse; fortunately he showed no interest so we were spared explanation.

His observation was still acute. It was good that I had only to cycle to the Training College with him once and know that he would get there safely on his own. He belonged to a boy scout troop and cycled off to the scout hut about two miles away every Thursday evening in all weathers. If he had had an accident he could have said who he was, but if asked his age would have been quite capable of replying with a garbled version of his address. We knew we were taking a chance on this dashing about on bikes, especially in winter when it was dark, but we had each other to share the responsibility and instinct urged us to encourage independence in him. He always had a piece of paper in his pocket on which my husband had typed out his name and address.

Going to Grandpa's farm was always a thrilling occasion for Freddy. He loved his grandparents, and he also loved Jack.

Jack was a man who had been on the farm even before my parents, and they went there when they married in 1920. He was tall and kind and infinitely gentle with Freddy. Ever since Freddy was able to walk, Jack had encouraged him to go with him on his various jobs and after a morning spent with Jack, the two would part with an arrangement to meet at a certain place at a certain time and often all Grandma's lunch arrangements would have to be altered because Freddy had a date with Jack. A lasting bond developed between these two.

Freddy was to have his first tweed jacket. We went to a store where they had a choice of about fifty, in all manner of tweed mixtures. Freddy went up to the row, took a careful look and picked out one in particular. It was his size and the only one in that tweed in that size. He would neither look at nor try on any other. 'Well Madam,' the attentive assistant said to me in a voice reverent with respect, 'he does seem to know his own mind and I'm sorry to tell you that this coat is one pound more than any of the others.' It was no good arguing and nothing would dissuade Freddy, so I paid up and smiled. When we got home I brought up the subject and asked him why it had had to be that one. Freddy replied firmly and quietly: 'It's like Jack's.' And Jack is still top of his Christmas present list of ten.

80

We had a birthday party for Freddy to which of course the gang came along with some other boys we knew, of an age we hoped he could cope with, including Ted, the boy from the house with the thick walls. We assembled Kim's game and I cheated by collecting together only objects that I knew Freddy was familiar with: a mousetrap, a piece of coal, a comb, a shoe, a match-box, etc. Twenty objects and a two-minute look and then the remembering and writing down. Freddy hid in a corner with me and told me what he remembered and I did the writing. He got seventeen. Almost all the other boys were defeated at twelve. We were delighted and not surprised and Freddy was pleased with himself which was nice on his birthday. It was his observation at work again.

But there were long stretches of the day when friends were not around, when the girls were either at school or with their friends or busy with their homework or practising, and Freddy was thrown back on his own resources. My husband had charge of a boarding house, and on the other side of a green baize door hummed the lives of sixty-six boys. I was kept busy on the outside edge of all this and often the affairs of those boys prevented me from doing things with Freddy. He was still passionate about Roman history and if no one was free to play with him, he would wander through the green baize door and get books from the boys' library.

He looked at any and every history book he could find on the subject and pored over the illustrations. From all this came a request, as summer drew on, to visit and walk down Hadrian's Wall.

No one else was particularly keen, though we all knew it was something we ought to have done and would be pleased about afterwards. So, come the summer holidays, we hitched up our newly acquired caravan and went. We parked in a deserted car-park about half-way between Newcastle and Carlisle. The wall snaked across Britain, undulating and impregnable. The country around was a shade of soft, wet green and the wild clouds threw enormous windy shadows over the deserted, reedy, sheepy terrain. We put on our gumboots and macintoshes and set off down the top of the wall. It was tough going, it switchbacked steeply down and up and we slithered about on the streaming clay. I think Freddy thought he was a Roman.

He took possession of the wall and set off on a six-mile

march to a museum he had seen in a book and was determined to visit. His father went with him but Jean and Heather and I knew that we were English and we returned to our camp for 4 pm tea.

The museum was a success and full of all the things he had been looking at in books for so long. He was absorbed with his Roman thoughts and was very happy. He had looked for coins all the way down the wall and on the return trip found what could well be a catapult stone, so we all felt the visit had been worthwhile. That night as we lay snug in our bunks the rain cascaded down and it made sweet music on the solid roof of the caravan just above our heads. I hugged myself in delicious decadence. We were warm and we were dry; tents were for France, caravans for England.

As the September term drew near, Dorothy began her speech therapy visits again and a visit to the hearing aid clinic gave us hope of a new aid made in Denmark and soon to be available in Britain, which was going to be a custom-built discriminating hearing aid, boosting only the frequencies he missed. This was a welcome revolution. We wondered how long we should have to wait as it was apparently going to fit snugly behind the ear and eliminate the wretched string which caught up in everything. By this time Freddy had been at the Junior School for a year. He was now twelve-and-a-half and moved up with his class to the nine-year-olds. It was just before Christmas that he had cause to write a letter about something, and I read what he had written and realized that in the three terms he had been at this school he had not improved in any way at all. One was tempted to say that nothing had been learnt. Time was flying by and his standing still on the academic front was alarming. The one burning question, what he was eventually going to do in the world, which everybody avoided asking and which we had always refused to think about ourselves, was very soon going to have to be faced.

We had refused to think about the time when he was going to have to earn his bread, for the very good reason that it was simply impossible. His development over the years had been so unpredictable that we had formed the habit of living (where Freddy was concerned) in each separate moment, sealed off

82

from the past or future. There were two levels of existence going on; our own lives and those of the girls in which exams were taken and careers plotted and plans made, and then our existence with Freddy which was a process of assessing each day and seeing where we were. He had started speechless and uncomprehending. He now spoke and understood many words and most situations. I could say to him that we were going camping and he would go and fetch his sleeping bag. He could tell me a friend had asked him to tea; he could not tell me which friend for certain and certainly not where any of them lived although he could have taken me there. He could never tell me at what time anything was to happen or what day, and he could not write things down. He was eager to go to the grocer's for messages and errands but as he could not contain the simplest item in his head, I always wrote a note for him to take. He could never manage the clearest instructions to a house in a street he was not familiar with, even with a drawn plan, and even when he added new streets to his ever enlarging repertoire, he could not connect names of people with streets they lived in, even people he knew well. He had a vast fund of detailed knowledge and a mass of historical facts which he was as yet unable to relate.

He crawled into his grandmother's bed early one morning and lay curled up in her arms gazing at her bedside lamp—a silver Corinthian pillar mounted on steps—and observed that it was Nelson's column. My mother was impressed, but amazed and bewildered by this exact observation. She felt it was good but how to use it? She fretted about this. I think she expected, she certainly hoped for, a smashing breakthrough. She wanted the clown to leap through the paper hoop, through the fire, and emerge to deliver a splendid oration to make sense of and to reward the energy which had been so exactingly expended on this accumulation of scattered facts. Freddy seemed so near the brink of total understanding and then she would find that despite his knowledge of Nelson, his navy and his column, she could not ask him if he would care to go to a skating rink that day for as she spoke the words 'skating' and 'rink' his face went blank—he did not know what she was talking about.

And so we lived our Freddy level of existence in a state of animation, joy, and despair—suspended. This suspension had become a way of life and in many ways it was vital escapism. We would jog along with Freddy, coping with the present as best we could, accepting with gratitude and wonder the steady progression from his past but stolidly refusing to take any great encouragement from this for the future because we knew too well what is expected and demanded of a whole person in the world today, and it was impossible to imagine how this child would cope with basic things like transport, post offices or asking and answering simple questions. As all this was impossible to imagine and very frightening, we donned our blinkers and carried on. It needed great jolts every now and again to shake us out of our groove and keep us awake at nights until we had thought up another and better way to get him a stage further on. We always got our jolts and Freddy's Christmas letter was one of them.

My husband was busy when I marched into his study without even knocking on the door and made my bold, bald, unquestionable and faintly hysterical statement, 'Freddy is not learning anything.' He replied 'I know he isn't and I haven't *time*.' This was just the spur I needed. Things were suddenly real again and my peaceful *un*realistic spell was at an end and action had to be taken. I remembered the nursery school he had attended at the age of four and I telephoned and poured out our predicament. Did they, could they, know of a teacher who could take him to tutor? I was asking the impossible. All good teachers were spreading their talent over the many and an old one would be past comprehending this strange, normal-looking but hiddenly complicated little boy. Anybody seeing the perfectly detailed aeroplanes and windmills and lighthouses he knocked up with his Lego bricks just would not believe there could be anything wrong here.

Three days later we heard that there was an experienced teacher who had been absent from teaching for two years while looking after her aged mother. This task had reduced her to a state of nervous exhaustion, and it was suggested that tackling Freddy was just what she needed to jolt her back into life. The aged mother had died, and if jolts were going to work two ways, this was going to suit us fine. Miss W came to see us one dark December afternoon.

She had on a heavy, plain, teapot-brown coat, strong serviceable shoes and an ancient felt hat. She didn't feel eccentric but she did look terrifically grey, and I suddenly felt most hopelessly defeated as we tackled the impossible task of trying to explain to her what Freddy was like. As my husband embarked on this exposition I watched Miss W and nothing at all appeared to register on this expressionless, seemingly blank pudding face.

Towards the end of the explanation, something my husband said suddenly made her smile. It didn't last long but just long enough to show a flash of warmth, sympathy and goodwill. It was not unbeautiful and it clinched the deal.

Freddy was signed off at the Junior School, Christmas came and went, the headmaster of a local private preparatory school for boys agreed to allow him to join them for afternoon games, which was vital if he was to have any life at all with other children apart from the once-a-week evening at the scout hut, and January dawned with Freddy cycling off to Miss W for Monday, Tuesday, Thursday and Friday mornings. Wednesdays were still spent at the Training College and so a new discipline began. Once again I tried to gauge Freddy's reaction to leaving yet another school. He had no feelings at all about it this time. He said he still wanted his friends and I reassured him that of course they should continue in his life. He said he only wanted to go to the 'two day' school and do some more 'moddlin'. I burned with resentment as he made this simple statement, my heart began to pound and I was shocked and frightened by a vicious desire within me, to find the people responsible, get hold of them and shake them till their teeth rattled. Love thine enemy. Comparatively easy if he hurts you, almost impossible when he attacks the defenceless.

I cycled with Freddy that first morning, and together we found Miss W's villa at the end of a quiet road. It was dark in her polished hall and the curling mahogany arms of her cloak-stand stood coatless and hungry against the beige wallpaper. There was a prize aspidistra in its brass pot at the foot of the narrow stairway on a fumed oak plinth beneath a secondary monarch of the glen.

But in the dining room, where morning sun streamed through a large window, life was brighter and there was a large picture of Bonzo with a litter of pink puppies in a basket. Miss W had a veritable exhibition of carefully chosen and attractive books

85

laid out on the table, looking much more inviting than any meal. Her aim for that morning was to peruse those books in an endeavour to find out what Freddy did and did not know in her terms. I left them together both looking slightly apprehensive, Miss W hesitantly determined, Freddy stubbornly resistant.

The first week passed. And so did a comment from Freddy, 'I don't like her.'

Me: 'Why?'

Freddy: 'She makes me do it.'

Me: 'Good, and about time too.'

And so another week passed with a rather cross Freddy sent forth on his bicycle each day. At the end of the second week we had a conference with Miss W. She said that in all her twenty-five years of teaching she had never met anything like this. We refrained from reminding her that we had warned her she was in for a surprise and she said she felt dreadfully inadequate and only wished she had had special training. We reassured her and told her that her discipline and insistence on a standard was in itself a good thing and that that alone would do for the time being, and that, anyway, we were quite sure *he* was picking up valuable knowledge even though she might feel *she* was getting nowhere.

The two terms he spent with her were interspersed with conversations which ran roughly on these same lines; she needed constant reassurance, Freddy settled, not unhappily, for the discipline though he kept up sporadic complaints on principle.

During one bout of moaning about Miss W I discovered that he had formed a private understanding with her old father who apparently took to shuffling past the dining room at intervals, slipping mintoes into Freddy's pockets. And one day when summer came and Miss W discarded her lisle stockings and sported her brown leather open sandals, Freddy huddled very close to me and whispered that he knew it wasn't her fault and that she couldn't help it but that he did not like her toes!

Meanwhile, my friend from the nursery school reported meeting Miss W's old father out shopping and he began thanking her most profusely for 'sending the boy along, for,' he said, 'Myrtle has started cooking again.' We too had noticed a change in Miss W; grey cardigans had turned to mauve and there had been one sunny Friday with some lipstick, so whatever was

86

happening to Freddy's education, at least something good was happening to her.

We decided Freddy should be confirmed. We liked our school chaplain, and he set about giving him most unconventional confirmation classes. A lot of drawing went on, and Freddy showed great interest. One day a visit was made to a church and interesting dark cupboards and little doors were unlocked and he was taught about the clothes and cups and things. Eventually the great evening came and Freddy knelt before the Bishop in Tewkesbury Abbey. The old priest who had given him spiritual healing so many years ago could not be with us in person but he knew of the day and the time. One godfather had died, and the other was in Yorkshire and could not come, and his godmothers both lived in South Africa, but they were all thinking about him that day. There was a friendly bun-gathering after the service and Freddy was proud and full of importance.

It was some time later when we were camping in Norfolk again that Freddy made an arrangement with the farm manager to go with him early to pick peas. We agreed to this on condition that he came quietly into the caravan and got his own breakfast. He agreed with alacrity and on his first pea-picking morning in he came, up before the sun. Through veils of sleep I could hear him being terribly quiet, but not for long. An opening and shutting of sliding plywood crescendoed to an unbearable pitch until through a yawn my husband said 'Freddy, what *are* you looking for?' Freddy, to our consternation, replied 'I've lost the Holy Spirit.' There was a pause, then my husband said 'Green tin, bottom left.' More plywood clatter and then silence. It was, of course, the Golden Syrup.

We often surprised ourselves with the degree of familiarity at which we had arrived in knowing what he meant. And though this incident was funny, it was also a salutary reminder of how deeply affecting impaired hearing is. It was the vowel sounds he caught, and the consonants he did not hear.

Another aspect of this incident occurred to us. What or who did Freddy think God was? To me, when small, He had been the Tailor of Gloucester in one of Mrs Tabitha Twitchet's best dresses. Was He to Freddy that sleeping lion with the bees buzzing round his head? It made us think seriously about schools for the partially deaf.

87

Dorothy, our speech therapist, thought that perhaps Freddy should be at one. The Hearing Clinic people had always said this. Yet we had never been drawn that way. However, Dorothy wrote to an old friend who had begun his career as a teacher of the deaf and was at that time serving on the inspectorate for special schools. This kind and understanding man saw us in his own home in London one Saturday afternoon. He went through all the tests for the deaf with Freddy and at the end of the consultation determined that he was *just* deaf enough to qualify for entry to a school for the partially hearing and said that he could recommend which one would be most suitable, but that we must be well aware that Freddy would be a big fish in a small pond and that there would not be the same challenge that there had been with him struggling at the Junior School. Added to this there was the ever-present danger of the protected environment again, and Freddy might well slide backwards in a sympathetic institution, with pressures removed, and perhaps collapse in a heap, from relief, and cease all effort. The final factor was the aphasia—although he was now considered almost *dysphasic,* that is, with only partial impairment of language. The teaching methods for the partially hearing did not include the techniques required for teaching the non-comprehending. Our friend sent us away to be our own jury and we decided against the school for the partially deaf.

Towards the end of the summer holidays, the miraculous discriminating hearing aid was made available. We went to London where 'Multitone' were cheerful, courteous and endlessly painstaking and made Freddy feel special and important. After a considerable time spent there, he emerged with this neat machine fixed behind his ear and with instructions about how to fit in the tiny batteries.

We had never looked upon Miss W as a permanency and our quest for schooling for Freddy continued. After mentioning our problem to another stranger, I received a telephone call from a friend of his giving me the name of an educational psychologist who had a reputation for successfully rehabilitating children into English schools after spells abroad with the Services, oil companies, etc. He was reputed to have made himself familiar with every kind of educational institution and all curricula. We wrote to him for an appointment. It was difficult for my husband to be away from his school during term-time but he was granted a day off and he went to great lengths to rearrange all his classes and browbeat a colleague into supervising his games in the afternoon. I confess to a built-in prejudice against psychologists and I felt it fully justified when at 10 pm the night before we were to go to see him, he telephoned saying he was in the throes of an attack of asthma, felt ill, was speechless and therefore we were not to come. My husband could not consider turning his life upside down a second time, so three weeks later Freddy and I went to London alone.

First the psychologist spoke to me and then went into a room where Freddy was perusing magazines and spoke to him. When he returned to speak to me again he described a school he knew in Sussex which he thought would suit Freddy well but which he knew had a formidable waiting list. He asked me the 64,000 dollar question about the future, to which I replied that I supposed Freddy must learn some trade but that these days it involved going to a technical college and I did not see how he was going to be able to manage listening to people speaking at speed, understanding or writing. He said that from his conversation with Freddy it appeared he liked books even though unable to read them precisely and he saw him working in a bookshop. I refrained from asking how he thought Freddy would cope with customers' change or invoices—particularly customers in a hurry—because it was a nice idea and I wanted to enjoy thinking about it. We parted with my asking him to write to the Sussex school to tell them about Freddy and to ask for their prospectus despite their waiting list.

8

And then the removal vans came and great changes took place in all our lives. Jean had left school the previous year, had done a short course of citizenship in London, stayed with cousins in South Africa and had spent nearly a year in Paris before embarking on a nursing career, and was now ensconced in a large children's hospital. Heather was at Edinburgh University reading an honours course in Spanish and French. My husband had resigned his post and had taken a temporary one, and this meant a move. Miss W had, through teaching Freddy, found new confidence away beyond mauve cardigans and announced her intention of going back to the profession full-time, so she could not have continued with Freddy. We had lived in our town for thirteen years and I for one was going to miss it dreadfully. The children had grown up there and in spite of everything that had happened, there was a lot I was deeply grateful for. Change is either growth or decay, and pinning our hopes on growth we set forth.

Over the actual move Freddy, Piglet-like, did a very brave thing. He went to stay with an elderly friend alone. This was something he had not done before. He had spent odd nights with David and Ted, but had never been away alone with a grown-up in surroundings he did not know and for several days.

Molly lived in a mill house in Oxfordshire. The mill itself did not work any more but everything there was still intact and it looked and felt as though the miller had only gone off for lunch and would soon return and get the wheel turning again. In the house was some very old furniture, in particular a bureau with a lot of small drawers all containing fascinating treasures, unbelievably tiny pairs of scissors and old stamps and other relics. Upstairs there was an Empire period bed and when Freddy arrived and saw it, recognizing the style from pictures he had seen in history books, he got the fixed idea that it was Napoleon's actual bed. Nothing would deter him from this conviction and we did not try as it seemed to us a harmless enough untruth, and when Molly said 'This is your room' and placed his case on the Holy bed, another friendship of the Jack style was established. This ambiance suited Freddy and he expanded in the warmth of the cultured security.

And then, it was time for some kind of school. Ever hopeful, we waited to see what our Authority was going to be like in our new county. The first step was a transfer of all Freddy's notes from the Hearing Clinic and we were called to see a specialist in a very new hospital. He put Freddy through all the tests and then said he wanted us to see another specialist in a large town in yet another county. We were dismissed and told that a letter containing instructions would come. We had no ideas, only the hope that there might be a special school which would meet our needs. We had moved to rurality and had a county education officer to deal with now instead of a borough one. There had been no further word from the big hospital so we contacted them. They were very angry with us because they said we had failed to appear at a consultation which had been arranged for us. As no correspondence of any kind whatever had reached us on this subject, people eventually cooled down and we were given an appointment to go the famous hospital in the next county.

Freddy and I saw a kindly ENT specialist who said the child's hearing loss must make life almost impossibly difficult and that there ought to be an aid in each ear. I saw my chance and asked if in his opinion a normal school could be the right thing for Freddy. He looked at me quizzically and asked me why I was asking such a stupid question. I explained that officialdom held this view, but that if he thought otherwise could he not give me a letter or make a report to this effect. He sighed and then explained that he was exclusively medical and had nothing to do with education and had no powers over any such authority, not even to advise. So we made an appointment to see Multitone in London again.

The existing hearing aid had been supplied by the National Health Service. If Freddy had one for the other ear, then the NHS would supply the old style box with the string. If we wanted another discriminating style, then we would have to pay. This seemed very fair to us, but £75 was a lot of money. In the end Multitone paid half. We shall never discover how or why. It was all very nice and they were unfailingly kind and encouraging. We never heard another word from that famous hospital, although the specialist had said he would want to see Freddy again, and then one day we read in *The Times* that our specialist had died.

Meanwhile we had been sent a prospectus of the school in Sussex recommended by the educational psychologist and also those of several other establishments. After careful study of them all, my husband was most attracted by the school which had been particularly recommended and we arranged a visit. It was situated in the Sussex Downs, with glorious views and perfect grounds. It was a mixture of buildings, a farm house and an old priory. The buildings had all been put to good use without spoiling their ancient character. A friendly labrador was prowling round and we left Freddy talking to him under some apple trees while we spoke to the headmaster. We had with us samples of Freddy's written work.

All we wanted to know was whether or not they felt they could help him with his education but this man talked endlessly on about their 'O' level achievements, the arrangements for games, some of the parents who were eminent in various fields and his very long waiting list. We tried to get him back onto the subject of Freddy's peculiarities but they were brushed aside and we were back with his own successes.

Was there something wrong with us? Were we doomed to stand before educationalists either unwilling to know or incapable of understanding what we were saying? As the familiar feeling of fatigue and depression set in and my head began to ache I wondered if this was how we were going to spend the rest of our lives. The spirit that used to make me want to throw things had turned to a dull and stubborn resistance to all teachers and schools.

I cut rudely across his talk, confronted him and asked him if he thought he could help and would consider taking Freddy. 'Oh yes,' came the easy reply and in an instant I knew he had not gleaned the faintest clue from the work we had shown him. We referred to this and asked him whether he had encountered such spelling and writing before and if he had any idea if it indicated a particular and possible approach to learning that he knew of. He implied that it was all quite normal to him and he made us feel he had met it all many times before. We knew he would get a big surprise.

We came away and Freddy announced as we swept through the gates that he liked the school and it was where he wanted to go. In spite of grave misgivings on some points we still thought this school had more to offer Freddy than any other we had heard of, particularly as the headmaster had said speech therapy would be arranged. So we wrote to him and asked him to give us the first possible vacancy. He held out little hope of one within a year.

We then heard that there was a class for the backward at the local secondary school. We were delighted, especially as Freddy had already joined the local scout group and if the town school was going to provide some education as well, then this was going to be a highly satisfactory state of thorough integration with our new surroundings.

I telephoned the headmaster and asked to see him. I explained briefly our situation and he suggested that Freddy and I came together. The buildings were new and beautiful and we were shown into a warm office. I began to explain how Freddy understood some things but by no means all and that aphasia still lurked. The headmaster heard me out and I was made to feel that I was yet another mother who knew her child was special and unique. He then said it would be better if we spoke to the teacher in charge of the class for the backward. This man was sent for and pulled up a wooden chair. As Freddy and I were sitting comfortably on upholstered chairs I made a sign to him not only to offer his chair to this man, but to insist that he take it. He reacted instantly but the teacher protested and insisted on remaining on his hard chair. Freddy became covered in confusion and half sat, half stood over his cushions, blushing profusely and not knowing how things had gone wrong. I found I could not talk about him and his problems with him there, and was very surprised that anyone else was prepared to. It seemed to me to be breaking all the rules of common sense and most basic psychology so I suggested to the two men that Freddy waited outside till the discussion was over. They both looked surprised and the headmaster said he could if I wanted, so Freddy was banished somewhere among the glossy 'two tone' corridors. I

93

then launched into my explanation, asking if they knew anything about aphasia and dyslexia. I met blank faces and apparent disinterest and the unspoken question 'Why are we all here?' seemed to hover in the air. I was the only person speaking. I wanted interest and questions and plans of campaign. The more these were unforthcoming the less I was able to stop talking and finally I stopped short in the middle of a statement about sums being meaningless to Freddy and asked the head if he could take him. 'Oh yes,' he answered coolly, 'he can come on Monday.' I said Freddy could cycle up and would he be kind enough to show him where he could put a bicycle and did he need any uniform? The teacher in charge of the backward class disappeared in a silent way; it was as if he had never been, and the headmaster led the way out of the door and we found Freddy in an office with a secretary.

He trotted beside me rather like Piglet, saying in an excited whisper, 'Isn't it grand?' and 'I've seen the gym' and 'the food smells nice.' We went out onto an area of tarmac and the head pointed to a bicycle shed. I thanked him for seeing us and said goodbye. Freddy said goodbye too and shot out a hand for a shake. The headmaster looked wildly round and after a long pause managed to produce a hand from behind his back which vaguely connected with Freddy's although the latter's was by this time in semi-retreat. We returned to the car and as we drove home I found it difficult to join with Freddy in his enthusiasm for his new school.

He set off the following Monday complete with black blazer, satchel and cap. He was a marked man from the start. It was odd joining the school two weeks after term had begun. It was odd to have plastic machines behind the ears and it was odd to be thirteen and small and in a special class. At this particular school it was apparently the oddest thing of all to say please, thank you and good morning and to open doors for people.

The class for the backward contained eleven children. Nothing was made exciting and the work was either too simple to take seriously or too difficult. At the end of each day I asked Freddy how he had got on and what he had done; he hated replying 'Oh noffin wealy', and would escape to his room and think about starting a new model and then find he hadn't the heart and would hang around bored, not liking himself or anyone else.

He had never been really bullied before. Every day blazer buttons were missing—I sewed on enough of them to have turned him into a Pearly King, had they all been on at the same time. He began to wear an aggressive and even furtive expression. We watched his spirits descend like the lift from the top of the Post Office Tower, the light went out of his eye and our next door neighbours who had been the joy of our lives since the day we arrived in our new town, with their endless kindness and interest, came round one morning and actually asked what had happened to Freddy. 'He isn't as nice as he used to be', they said.

My immediate reaction to this question was one of blind fury. A thousand replies came to my lips and it wasn't handbags that were in danger of flying but sharp claws. I counted ten slowly and then said 'Yes it does show, doesn't it,' and later that evening, much later, I was able to feel grateful to them for delivering the jolt we always got, but the mere thought of more necessary action so soon was too much. We waited. Each day we hoped for things to go better but they didn't, and it was no fun watching Freddy eat his breakfast, sling his satchel over his shoulder, say goodbye in a flat voice, turn and walk heavily and with slovenly steps out to school.

One evening he came back with a buttonless and torn blazer, threw his satchel on the kitchen floor and, scarlet in the face, said 'It's no good Mum, I *like* histowy and I want to listen but the teacher just stands there and says Shut up! Shut up! Shut up! all the time' and he burst into tears. He didn't actually burst, but his tears began to fall in a seemingly endless flow. They were bitter silent tears, as deep as the ocean and as dark as the grave. I pulled him to me and sat on a chair with him on my knee and together we rocked and rocked.

I don't know how long we stayed that way.

Time became eternity and I don't remember what happened next; it was probably beans on toast and ice cream. What I do remember and know is that if there had not been the backing of our family and our friends who were all so concerned for us, I would have given way to final disillusion and nervous catastrophe then. But there was also that inner inexplicable knowledge gleaned in Cornwall in the rain, when something had happened, and this set-back must therefore be a stone in the hoof, call it what you will, but not the END.

95

Next morning our subdued Freddy set out as usual and then the post arrived and there was a vacancy for him at the school in Sussex for the very next term. We shall never know how we got it and I don't know how I got through that day. The clock people were back at their tricks and it took a fortnight to reach four o'clock. There was a rush of cold wind, the door slammed and Freddy came in. 'Tell me, darling,' I said, 'what is the very best thing that could happen?' There was a long pause.

'Going to Grandma's?'

'No.'

'New tyres on my bike?'

'Oh no, *think!*' I said, 'Something you want more than anything else, something we *all* want.'

'Not,' he said, hesitantly, hardly daring, 'that school?'

'Yes,' I said and this time it was I who cried. Freddy's face was a study. He started to laugh, we danced, I grabbed a tea-towel from the Aga rail, rolled it into a ball and we threw it about.

'When?' he cried.

'Next term' I sang and then we both got the giggles. Next term! Next term! It wouldn't have mattered if we had had nothing to eat for supper that night but fortunately my husband was home and hungry and that brought us down to earth. We began celebrating all over again but in a more sober fashion and we all indulged in remembering the view of the downs and the dog and the hockey pitch and the nice dormitories and that we were going to be near Granny again.

'And,' said Freddy, 'I shall be able to go and see them at my first school.' He had never forgotten those far-off days at the John Horniman school. Neither had we.

9

After all this emotion we were rather brisk with Freddy next morning and very careful to see that he was well on time for school and a short rather sharp lecture was delivered by my husband that he was to finish his term there well and there was to be no slacking just because he was going to leave, and most important of all, he was to say nothing to anybody about it.

I was fairly brisk with myself too, and wrote to the Education Authority saying we had found a school which we felt could further Freddy's education better than the present one and would they send him there? We maintained that it was their responsibility to educate children in their care and that if this necessitated boarding, then those fees should be assessed by a means test. The answer came back that the education already being provided was adequate. We replied that we did not agree, that the child was backward, certainly, but that he was also intelligent, that there was no apparent attempt being made to stretch these children with their limited ability either to the utmost or even to their individual limits and that therefore they, the children, were losing out on the deal.

There was a silence of some two weeks and then a doctor was sent to our home. He came with the minimum of warning, after school, and hastily put Freddy through the basic medical hoop.

The board with letters on it for testing eyes, a rather sketchy hearing test which was an insult to the patient people in the Hearing Clinics who had spent so much time testing Freddy over the years, a thump on the chest, some questions to us, and with a sharp snap of the clasps on his black bag he was gone.

We wrote again to the Authority requesting approval for his attendance at the school in Sussex and they replied that the medical report confirmed their view that the education already provided was adequate.

We wrote back reminding them that Freddy and other children like him needed not only a special class but speech therapy and teachers trained to teach partial hearing complications and other defects.

They replied that teachers of the deaf and speech therapists were provided and visited the schools regularly. This last statement had us completely bewildered as we knew that no such people had put in an appearance at Freddy's school.

We wrote to this effect and at some point in the lengthy correspondence someone gave the game away by admitting that all these facilities were on paper.

We were back in the thick of Kafkaland and this time I could really let myself go, because we were opting Freddy out of it all. He was going to the school that did not know the degree of hopes it held for us, so he was all right, but what about everyone else? I wrote a direct and passionate letter to the Authority demanding one thing and one thing only, some *honesty*. I told them that I felt they were taking our requests as personal criticism which was, of course, ridiculous as we were well aware of costs and that the government of any country could hardly be expected to have schools on hand for every type of child, but that this was no reason for saying that what was available was *right* for every child. I said it was a mistake to divorce theory from reality and that for those in dire need, specialized teachers and therapists visiting schools in principle and on paper was something very different from them never actually materializing.

The resulting change of attitude was alarming. Very elaborate arrangements were made for Freddy to attend a Health Clinic in the town on a certain morning during school holidays where he could receive some speech therapy. We accepted this offer with gratitude and relief and as the half-term holiday was coming up we made certain not to miss any of these sessions.

I felt decidedly ill at ease. Freddy was getting some speech therapy but were arrangements like these made for others? The subject of visiting teachers for the partially deaf and speech therapists was not mentioned in the letter, and we forebore to press the point. We were, in fact, so incensed by the way things were done, the autocratic attitude and the ensuing unconcern for the individual children, that we wrote once again about the school in the South.

I think the Authority was tired of us by this time and felt that in providing us with speech therapy they had done as much as anyone had a right to expect. Their reply was curt. It stated that investigations had been made and that even if they had the means, even if they considered the child in need of special education, nothing would induce them to spend public money on this school as it was not recognized. This puzzled us somewhat, as it had been so well recommended by a recognized educational psychologist, and we wrote to the headmaster for a clarification of this situation. He replied that it was true the school was not recognized since it had not yet qualified in terms of time, only having been in existence for four years, but that it was registered.

This gave us something to think about. We couldn't see how a school could be registered without being automatically recognized. Why were there these confusing differences and what were they? I was beginning to wake in the night unable to sleep again.

It looked as though there was some constructive education coming up for Freddy, but I was haunted by the knowledge that a lot of children in need were sitting in those classes for the backward, unextended, bored and listless. It occurred to us that there were probably some ESN children in the class. In rural areas such as ours, special 'anything' is rare and whereas there may well have been an ESN school in the one large industrial town nearby, it would come under a different Authority and therefore the rural children would not qualify for entry.

Where then were the ESN children in the county getting their schooling? Surely everyone has sympathy for the ESN child and its problems and even more for its parents and I felt it was just as important that these children had the benefit of adequate facilities as the likes of Freddy, but ESN is a very different condition from backwardness and the two should never be mixed. The teaching techniques are quite different for the two conditions and very much more can and should be got from a backward child than can or should be expected from one who is ESN.

In Freddy's class for the backward, nothing was demanded of the children except that they should shut up, and the ensuing demoralization as seen in Freddy under this rule was very alarming indeed. He needed mental discipline and the challenge of a standard to strive for, sympathy, patience and understanding of the anathema of maths and allied subjects and encouragement,

lots of it, for the things that could be mastered. All he did get was
'Shut up!'

What are our children like if they get 'Shut up!' from eleven
till fifteen years of age? Has society any cause to complain and
shake its head in condemnation, if a large number of youngsters
reject society and turn in on themselves and demonstrate their
rejection with too much or too little hair? Who has ever made
them feel that anybody cares? A family, loving, indifferent or
neglectful, isn't enough. We all need to be accepted by society.
Is a school time of 'shut upping' an ideal or good way for a
growing person to develop confidence and self-respect?

I wasn't living very well on my shortage of sleep so I gave
myself a dose of 'shut up' and I wrote to the national press. For
my victim I chose a well-known columnist from the paper I read.
He was a past-master at exposing nonsenses and was no lover
of bureaucracy and I felt confident he would carry my banner
for me. His reply was prompt and kind but he said there was
nothing he could do; though he did say he had sent my letter
on to the Educational Correspondent of the same paper. I never
heard from him and looked in vain for any relevant articles. I
also wrote to *Woman's Hour*.

Being someone who never seems to learn, I again flung our
problem at the feet of the principal of an educational institution
nearby. He was highly professional and of some standing in the
educational world and I was certain he would care. By this time
I felt I was fighting for a cause, and my mind was filled with
concern for all the children in Britain missing out on vital
training. I was concerned also about the worry and stress suffered
by parents and I wanted everyone in the country to be aware
too, and get things changed.

He and his wife listened to me patiently and seemed mildly
interested, but I suddenly knew that they were not interested
enough to do something. I suffered a blow of great disappointment as I felt that as an educationist, let alone as a person, this
man would be bound to feel something could be done and I
was relying on his brilliant mind to think up what.

They were both very busy people and in the public eye and no
one can be all things to all men. I felt a fool for having set such
store on the certainty of there being an answer for me here. Once
again I had misjudged my educationists and, covered in con-

fusion and embarrassment for wasting their time and feeling flustered and self-conscious about my 'cause', I beat an ignominious retreat. I could not decide whether I had been talking to people with compassion but no understanding, or understanding and no compassion. I felt quite certain it was one or the other and possibly the former, like poor George Orwell who tried to fly the flag for the exploited miners in Lancashire with deep compassion but no real understanding of their actual problems at all.

Eventually I made an appointment to see the local MP. It took a long time to meet this busy man because he was always being called away on urgent business whenever my turn came round. When this had happened a third time, in desperation he telephoned me and simply said 'I'm so sorry to keep missing you, tell me all.' I asked him if he had three-quarters-of-an-hour to spare and warned him we would be lucky if we were through by then, even going flat out. He said 'Have a try.'

At the end of it all he asked me to put everything I had said on paper in a letter to him, and he would certainly take the matter up. We were much encouraged by this and some time later he asked me to come to his office one Saturday morning.

He said he had spoken to the then Minister of State for Education and had watched her read all of my letter. For a stunning moment with my heart pounding I saw a glorious future of instant reform. Special schools in rows in every town and no more heartache and despair for countless thousands of children and parents, problems realized, understood and accepted by all . . . The MP was speaking—'She finished the letter and then said "Oh yes, we are aware of dyslexia and communication-problem children and there are blueprints in hand for special schools, but you know how long these things take." '

I said to the MP 'Yes?' questioningly. He rather felt the interview to be at an end and the subject closed but I had barely begun. 'The point is,' I said, 'we all know about plans and how long they take but if, in the meantime, while all these buildings and policies are being argued about, someone tires of waiting and starts a school, and such a school can be found to be helpful to a problem child, should it not be used until such time as the government is able to provide? The answer the Minister gave after reading my letter was no answer.'

Our MP wavered a moment and then agreed. From that time on he was tireless on our behalf, became interested in the whole subject and finally put down a question in the House of Commons about the education of children with speech and hearing disorders. I quote the reply to his question: 'Special schools and classes are provided for children with impaired hearing and separately for children with speech defects not caused by deafness. Teachers of the deaf or speech therapists, as appropriate, help children with these disabilities also in regular classes of ordinary schools. An enlargement of Moor House School for children with severe speech defects is planned and a residential school for non-communication children is expected to open in the near future in Manchester.'

This was another non-answer and in true Irish fashion (without apologies) teachers of the deaf and speech therapists apparently practise their profession in all our schools whether they are there or not.

We thanked the MP for taking all this trouble and he agreed with us that it was a thoroughly unsatisfactory state of affairs.

Term ended and Freddy brought his books home. Ten out of ten for *everything,* including some work bearing spelling mistakes which he himself noticed and pointed out as we went through it all. He made it quite plain that to him the flattering marks were meaningless and a more misguided form of encouragement we felt would have been difficult to find. They had patronized Freddy with those silly marks and he just shrugged his shoulders in disdain.

10

It was January, Christmas had come and gone, and it was time to buy uniform for Freddy's new school. We bought a trunk, and with that and a bicycle we set off. The school was welcoming and friendly. Freddy was confident and glad to see the dog again. Dogs were everywhere in his life except at home. When we made our move we had asked Freddy if he wanted a dog of his own and explained that he would have to feed it himself and take it for walks everyday. He considered all this and let the subject drop. It seemed he was happy to settle for the dogs on his grandfather's farm and 'other people's', in general.

We had a short interview with the headmaster and tried to explain again Freddy's particular problems. We warned him that he still got muddled over time and the names of meals, that he could not be relied upon to understand orders or take messages and that he was still relying to a large extent on his sight, where perception was sharp. We asked him to oversee his pocket money and advise on careful spending as this was a field in which Freddy had had until very recently no experience, it being impossible to explain relative value in cash terms.

This man listened to us patiently. My husband explained the situation so clearly and while he was doing so I tried to imagine what I would have made of it all had it not been known to me, but I could not and I got a strong impression that the headmaster was not taking in and working, in his own mind, on the very important things my husband was saying. My built-in resistance to all schools and teachers was increased when with some impatience I distinctly detected a note of patronage in his manner which I felt he believed was giving reassurance. Could he be relied upon to tell his tiny staff to exercise extra patience and do their very best to train Freddy to do rudimentary sums? Would he appreciate the need for a standard and an insistence on good order and purpose? We could only hope and referred to the promised speech therapy and explained that this should come from the Local Authority. We then went off to see the matron and explain about hearing aid batteries.

Later that term when we had gone down to see Freddy and discovered that he had not been having any sessions in speech therapy, we reminded the headmaster of our request and how very important it was and he replied that the Local Authority were not willing to provide this service. We could only presume it was something to do with the school being registered but not recognized and could not face an argument, so we settled for the holiday sessions at home. These shortly came to an end as the happy, helpful person to whom Freddy had been proudly announced that she was expecting a baby in the summer. Whether or not she was replaced by somebody else we never discovered; no one ever informed us or suggested Freddy continued in another town or area, or anything.

The leaves were turning the following October when I went back to our old town for an evening's discussion on censorship in general and literature in particular. Among the literary, journalistic and television personalities on the platform was one of the writers who had stayed with us eleven years previously.

This was Gillian Freeman. We met in the crush in the bar after the discussion and almost the first thing she said was 'How is that little boy?' I replied that he was, with luck, going to be reasonably all right. How, without good reading, with unintelligible writing and a lot of non-comprehension, we did not yet know; it had all been so difficult for so long that we could barely see anything objectively any more. I added that we had discovered vast areas of deprivation and dishonesty in our educational system and that we were deeply concerned. She suggested I meet her the following month to talk.

This I did, and went up to London to her home. We ate our lunch and talked about all our children, the books she had written, the film scripts she was writing, their recent trip to America, and the enterprise my husband was hoping to embark on when his temporary job came to an end. After lunch we cleared both the lunch things and our minds and got down to the business of Freddy.

I have never found it easy to relate experiences or explain

104

situations clearly and concisely and I always weave my accounts into great sagas because of the fascinating but irrelevant details with which I clutter my life. Often my articulation is so bad that I have sometimes wondered if the only thing wrong with Freddy is the fact that he is *my* son! I tried very hard to be concise and Gillian sat silent, listening and occasionally asking wholly comprehending questions. It was such a relief to be with someone with whom I did not need to deviate with copious extra explanations, with someone who succeeded in projecting herself so well into our situation that I began to feel quite light-headed. Gillian was listening and thinking and not having her own ideas and theories. She wasn't 'knowing better' and this was a rare experience for me. At the end of it all she asked me to arrange in chronological order and then send to her all our correspondence on Freddy, and she promised to go through it and write an article which she hoped to have accepted by the *New Statesman.*

I thanked her from depths in my heart I did not know I had, and went home. As always, after telling anyone about Freddy in detail, I was enveloped in a huge sombre cloud of anxiety. Talking was an escape into words from the actuality of him. It was often strangely exciting, but after all had been spilled out I was left with a yawning aching greyness stretching into the unknown and unknowable future and always accompanied by a splitting headache.

I caught my train in this state of hot-cold, low-high nervous depression and kept myself carefully to myself in my corner seat because whenever I got like this I cried so easily, and though I cried *for* Freddy I always felt I had let him down when it happened. On this occasion it was my heart that was crying and it was because Gillian really cared and because so many other people did not. Her concern threw into relief the inhuman indifference shown by the 'experts'. She was at least as busy as they, yet she was going to make time to back our cause with her pen.

My husband and I spent the following weekend sorting out the correspondence and, registered and costing £1 in postage, Freddy's life was dispatched.

Gillian's article came out in the spring and just before it did so, we received our last communication from the County

Authority. It referred to the flashing visit made by the doctor the previous year and stated that they would like another of their MOs to see Freddy during the Easter holidays 'so that we can keep in touch with him and see whether there is any further help we can offer.' We could not think what the previous 'help' had been to which they so firmly referred as we were not aware of having been offered any at all, but we let them come, and after the visit they were never seen or heard of again.

The article was the Centrepiece in the *New Statesman*. All schools, educational authorities and in some instances people were clearly mentioned by name. There were no repercussions from any authority. Perhaps they knew we had corroborating evidence in every letter they had ever sent. Interested people were very glad it had been printed. Some people still seemed to think it was all a bit of a fuss about not very much. A few could not believe we had had so much bother. Only one person, the chairwoman of a children's committee, asked what the effect of it all had been on the child.

About a week later an article appeared in *The Times* which referred to 'the eloquent case made by Sir Alec Clegg in a twelve-page document—*Waste of Human Potential in Education*'. He estimated that only 5,000 of the 35,000 children in the West Riding who needed special education were receiving it. Not all these children were of course suffering from the same complaint as Freddy. But to me the significant thing was that here at last was a chief education officer honest enough to admit a shortage of vital amenities in his province. I wrote to him and thanked him and asked him if he had seen the *New Statesman* article about Freddy. He replied and showed interest.

A week or two later I received the following letter from the mother of a speechless five-year-old. She had seen Gillian's article and had written to her. Gillian sent the letter on to me :

Thank you for your most informative article in this week's *New Statesman*. Until today I had thought that we were unique in having a child who cannot be 'labelled'. My five-year-old daughter cannot speak more than about ten words and has severe behaviour disorders as a result of this handicap. To date she has been seen by : deaf specialists, ENT specialists, the late Dr John Yudkin, three educational psychologists,

106

the Borough's mental health doctor, Dr X of Sunfield Homes (Steiner School), two faith healers, a witchcraft coven, and a speech therapist at UCH. We have been offered no advice whatsoever from any of these sources (other than the speech therapist who feels that a Steiner school might be the answer) and are waiting for a place for her at a junior training centre where I am quite sure she will be unhappy, and sink to a very low level mentally. You say in your article that Freddy was sent to a well-known special school, can you please tell us *how*? As I understand it, a child has to be recommended by its own MOH for a place at a residential school and our Borough could not be more tight-fisted or apathetic about retarded children. I should be most grateful to be put in touch with the parents of Freddy, whose case seems identical with that of K. After the strain of caring for her at home for five years I am nearly at breaking point but the possibility of contacting someone who may be able to give concrete advice has given me new hope. Also have you any information about the residential school in M . . . which was also mentioned in your article? I should mention that nearly all the people who have seen K have said that if she was autistic, epileptic, spastic or more deaf than she is, she could be placed fairly easily at a school catering for these handicaps.

I wrote to the writer of this letter and asked if she would like to come with the child to see me.

I collected them from a station ten miles away in pouring rain. The little girl was not trained and had obviously been obstreperous all the way down in the train. I could see that the mother was strained and despairing and very, very tired of the child as she was. I was worried by the child who did not resemble Freddy at the same age in any way. She appeared to have no concentration and when I put out some toys for her she showed no interest. Sometimes I was sure she knew what she was doing and was playing up, but it was difficult to be certain. They were having all our later educational problems now. Nobody ever questioned Freddy's aphasia once it was diagnosed but these poor people could not get their Authority to acknowledge the condition.

During the course of our discussion about the problems created by the child, the mother told me an extraordinary thing. She said the child once came into their sitting room, saw a tumbler which had some neat whisky in it, drank it all straight off and then said a complete sentence in a perfect take-off of the mother's voice. I was fascinated by this. I asked her if she had told any doctor and said I felt she should and that it could be very important to anyone doing research on the subject. Obviously the stimulation of the whisky released something. I wished I knew more about metabolism. Had the whisky got straight into the blood circulation and did that take a one-way route to the brain? I felt sure that someone ought to know about this, as the child was quite speechless when sober.

There wasn't a single moment during the visit when the mother and child seemed able to relax and have any enjoyment or satisfaction in each other's company. It just didn't appear possible under the circumstances. No sooner had I laid the table for our lunch than the knives and forks had been sent spinning by the wildly waving arms of the child. All the way to the station at the end of the afternoon, she sat on her mother's knee in the front of our car and her arms had to be held in an iron grip to prevent those little hands making for the gear-lever, the window-wiper knob, the ash tray, anything she could pull, push or make move. The only advice I could give was to try to get her into the John Horniman school and of course I armed the mother with the address and telephone number, and she promised to let me know how she got on.

Six months later I was writing to another mother in search of the right answer to her problem. She had seen Gillian's article and lived on a farm in Yorkshire. I quote her reply:

Dear Mrs—

Thank you so much for writing to us. I would have written back sooner had I not felt it would be better to wait until after our visit to Professor —, head of the Audiology Department at Manchester University. Timothy was seven years old on June 21, 1968. From two weeks old he did not appear to be aware of the very loudest sounds. He was always very happy but had weeks at a time when he seemed to 'stare' and 'dream'. He was always very painfully constipated despite the suitable food, or the laxatives which we gave to him.

He seemed to be able to hear any sound which was a 'new

sound' and we felt so many times that he could not be deaf. However, a local specialist thought that he might be and we started with weekly lessons with a peripatetic teacher and we were to help him.

This did not do any good, amplification seemed to make him worse, although he could stand it for quite long periods. When he was almost four years old I took him to London, to the Grays Inn Road hospital. I stayed three weeks, instead of the usual one week, in a valiant effort by the staff to find out how deaf he was, if deaf at all. They did suggest that our Education Authority buy a Philips hearing aid. They would not do this without instructions from Manchester University. So back we went. Timothy was given an EEG test. Wires were glued round his head and he was tested when asleep.

This resulted quite differently again. M —, the Lecturer in Clinical Audiology gave many hours watching Timothy and the EEG showed that 'Any hearing loss that there may be did not cause the language disorder.' In those days we thought that time would cure him. To a large extent time has shown long, slow improvement.

In February this year Timothy spent a week at Moor House —result 'not unlike a deaf child, not unlike an aphasic child.' In May Timothy and I spent a week at the new Ewing School for Aphasic Children. Result—deaf. This term he is spending at the Northern Counties School for Deaf Children, Newcastle. He is happy there.

Last Wednesday we went back to Manchester. Professor — tested and said 'profoundly deaf'. Today I have a letter from the headmaster saying that Timothy is not responding to high amplification, shows no signs of lipreading, shows a profound hearing loss and a specific disorder of communication.

I think that I have taught Timothy most of what he knows (i.e. reading, counting). He is a very happy, affectionate and bonny little boy, anyone not knowing him thinks him shy when he smiles but does not speak.

Our daughter Rosemary is eleven years old, David ten years old and Nicholas one year ten months.

I wonder if you have other children and if your son resembles Timothy at all. Timothy can copy vowel sounds and coughs for sharp sounds.

I went to their farm and we had a long discussion about their son and after all the conflicting advice they had received he seemed to be happy and settled at his school for the partially hearing in Newcastle, so although they were by no means convinced that deafness was his problem or that he was at the right place, they were rather helplessly settling for it.

Much later a third letter came. As the article was by this time eighteen months old, I could only presume this person had brought her chips home in it and read through the smudges of vinegar and grease. I was filled with curiosity. It read thus:

Dear Miss Freeman,

In April of last year I was very interested to read an article by you in the *New Statesman*, concerning the difficulties in finding appropriate education for a boy.

I am now writing to ask your assistance as I have a similar problem, as I am now in despair of ever finding a school for my son Michael, now exactly ten years old. He is minimally brain-damaged and has the additional disadvantage of being fatherless, as my husband died suddenly when he was two years old.

In your article you mentioned a private school in the south, for boys with IQs between 70 and 100 (Michael on the WISC scored 91 on the verbal scale and 69 on the performance scale). I wondered whether you could give me further information about it or any other facilities which you have discovered. I may say that I wholly share the frustration of the parents in your article. My son has made negligible progress in his present school, recommended by the Local Authority; but responded dramatically to a minimal amount of private coaching, which I instituted recently. Unfortunately this is only for two hours a week, compared with the twenty or more classroom hours, but it does prove that he is at present working far below his potential, and that the school does not offer the right stimulus.

I should be most grateful for any help you can offer. I enclose a stamped addressed envelope for your reply.

I called to see this woman. We talked for a long time and compared our problems and difficulties, and when I left I felt the most helpful thing I had done was to give her the name and address of the educational psychologist who had sent us to Sussex. Before leaving, I asked about the chips. But she told me that in the midst of a busy working life and the worry and complications and time involved in coping with her son and everything else, she had, with the help of friends, accumulated every article they ever saw relating to handicapped children. It had taken all these months slowly working through the articles before reaching ours.

II

Freddy attended the Sussex school for two years. On arrival he had formed an instant attachment to the matron, discovered she had a passion for Mars bars and made himself responsible for keeping her supplied from the village shop. He went there on his bicycle, carefully clutching her money, and it kept him busy as she took a trip with Mars every day.

He liked his school. He threw himself into hockey playing. He made friends with the Irish chef and the man who taught woodwork, and was accepted by the other boys. He did not make any close friends. He went for very long walks alone on the Downs. He learnt to ride. There was a good riding school nearby and several boys used it. Freddy was learning from scratch. He took to it like a duck to water. They had a covered school and he was taught the basics in horsemanship. He spoke of it during his holidays as if it was something he had done all his life. He revelled in the collective companionship of the other boys and responded to community living. Once he had found out the form, when bells rang, he knew what they meant and happily reacted to their every clang. He gained in social confidence and only when our questions turned to his class work did he show signs of uncertainty. I quote one of his letters :

Dera Mum and Dad,

Thank you for your letter Mum. I was carly unerstoad of your peplaise about the journey horne at half-terom I am alfrwy sorry about borthrug you to see the people in londun but I know what to say to those abit my other heraid which hurts my ear and the repair but it does not seem to work so well whe I put it in my ear so I am going to tell Matron about it tomorrow mornin I had a nice time withjen tooday and I had got a news and I met jene and had lunch which was nice and then went to Mursing home and then we went on the pire and had a candy flose. Best love Freddy.

My husband being unable to get away from school, Heather and I went down for one of the Open Days held during the summer terms and Jean joined us from her hospital nearby. I tried to find out about Freddy's progress. We judged his English work by his letters but it was difficult to get a clear picture of the other subjects from the various masters because they were all warmly, vaguely encouraging, obviously liked Freddy but would not be pinned down when questioned in detail about the work.

Because I am not an educationist, I did not feel qualified to criticize the school's display of work and activities, but as all the boys suffered from some ailment or other that hindered them from coping with formal education in schools provided by the government or private bodies, my instinct told me there should be an emphasis on art and drama to help the inarticulate or psychologically confused child to express himself. I saw no sign of either. I knew I must leave this for my husband to tackle when he fetched Freddy at the end of term. This he did, and seemed reasonably satisfied with the replies he received.

For the time being, Freddy was having such a good time being with boys of his own age with whom he felt he could cope, and it was doing him so much good, that we relaxed into a dream and let it ride.

Another letter from Freddy read as follows:

Dea Mum and Dad
    Thank you for your letter. I have been out to lunch with Grany today and it was lovely and I had won two games. Black Gamon and the spellig one which was fun and I had the scor of 226 or more because I can't rember the eviry number. I know this is erly to asked who is cominig too colected me at the half term, so please let me know and I think it is importunt to me I am wrightig to Grany now so goodby untell next week.

Freddy spoke as he heard and wrote as he spoke. He certainly communicated. We wondered if anyone at the school was making suggestions about punctuation. Sentences such as 'I wordert mind of I had a book tokin and because I am vealy interested in the Royal Navy that I wornt mind to get one from my book tokern for Christmas, the girls can give me a model of the

Bistmon a second world war war ship' were typical. *We* all understood exactly what he meant because we knew it all so well, but after the Christmas referred to in the letter, Freddy was going to be fifteen, and if we had not had the means with which to keep him at this school where we still hoped progress would be made, he would be leaving then and having to make his way in the world.

In spite of his interest in the Royal Navy and the *Bismarck* and all the other useful bits of know-how he was collecting from his life in Sussex, like mending fuses and bicycle punctures and other basic 'boy' activities, there was still no question of his travelling across London on the Underground alone. A main-line train could be risked with someone to put him on at one end and someone else to get him off at the other, but he was some way off mastering the intricacies of the tube trains and there was always the non-comprehending problem.

If Freddy spoke to a person who did not at first understand what he had said, provided that person was patient and sympathetic and asked Freddy to repeat himself, then he could generally make himself understood in the end. On the other hand, there was no guarantee that he would understand the replies of the person correctly. It required confidence he did not have, to ask grown-ups, and strangers at that, to repeat themselves, and anyway they might not understand *that* request! We felt the time was some way off when we should be able to let Freddy travel alone with any degree of confidence. The Sunday horror-paper hazards which exist for any small boy on his own are always there, and Freddy had a friendly disposition and would speak to anyone and everyone at the drop of a hat, bag or brolly.

But these were not the only risks, and the complications that could have occurred were kaleidoscopic possibilities of arrivals at improbable destinations, in view of 'Lewes' and 'Pewsey' sounding the same to him; Hertford and Dartford; Manchester and Lancaster; Dulwich and Norwich. He would have confused Newmarket with Market Harborough and he could not have understood at all about Stratford East and the one upon the Avon. And he could not yet manage a public telephone.

So the Sussex school saw him onto a train for Victoria and we got him off. It was usually a very early train at the end of term and in case of accidents he knew how to go to the big hotel and wait in the foyer, and my husband saw that he always had a typed notice explaining who he was and why, in case a hall porter queried his presence and Freddy did not understand.

The school was very keen on projects and Freddy attempted several good ones and collected a lot of general knowledge. Nevertheless at the end of his first year there were still alarming gaps yawning and no one seemed to be properly tackling sums. Added to this, a simple request that he be encouraged to attend Holy Communion services, which he had done regularly since the great Confirmation day in Tewkesbury Abbey, was not adhered to and when we enquired of Freddy if he ever went to the little local church for Communion, he replied that a prefect came round taking the names the night before the service and that the prefects had always laughed when he had put his name forward and refused to believe that he had been confirmed and that there the matter had ended. His confirmation had been discussed with the headmaster. It did seem that no one ever thought anything we told them mattered.

My husband had several academic talks with the masters from time to time. They all stated a liking for Freddy, which was gratifying, but continued strangely vague when pressed to give an opinion on his attainments in book-work. There was no sense of urgency and a decided lack of thought about the future which lurked forbidding and too close for comfort.

At the end of the summer term, which was Freddy's fifth, we discovered from his report that he had not been doing any history. We could not believe it. We asked him if this could be true, and if so then why, particularly as it was his favourite and best subject. His answer was simple: 'Well Mum, the master uses a tape-recorder all the time and I can't lip-read a tape-recorder.'

I was overcome by an old familiar feeling. It began at the top of my head and felt like pins and needles. It spread slowly, all over me, downwards. Unbelievably, but once again it seemed the game was up. I said nothing of this to my husband because there was no need. I knew he knew. The summer holidays began. Heather returned from a holiday in Spain, and after three days in the house with Freddy came to me and said 'Mum, Freddy isn't learning anything.'

'You don't have to tell me,' I replied. 'We *know*.'

My husband was especially busy at this time and I could not keep on discussing it all with him, although there was nothing else I wanted to do. This new old situation took its usual control of my life. As when one is in love, it dominated every thought and action. I cooked and cleaned and arranged flowers and carried on conversations with people and made shopping lists and organized picnics and went to the cinema, and all the time I thought of nothing except how to get Freddy a little bit further educated before he faced the world.

In fairness to all we felt we must make a big effort to discover why and how this highly recommended private school was failing us. So we made a careful list of questions to take to Sussex as we very much wanted a full talk with the headmaster to find out in precise terms his summing up of Freddy's prospects. Very interesting it was. All our criticisms were acknowledged—that there was no demand for excellence, no sense of urgency or excitement, no attempt to tackle sums and no history. The headmaster agreed that Freddy was someone who thrived on challenge and had a healthy regard for people who demanded a standard and he also agreed that he was getting neither.

This, he went on to explain, was because the other boys at the school were all suffering from various forms of resistance to any kind of pressure. He had there, he said, boys who, when told firmly to produce work by a certain time, began throwing ink pots or fits, or who got into a 'state'. He also had boys who would recoil and become disturbed at the sight of a blackboard and formal rows of desks. This was the reason for all the lessons taking place with chairs placed informally round the teacher.

There were boys who were unable to take in anything spoken to them directly but who were perfectly susceptible to an impersonal voice from a tape-recorder. All this made sense to us in view of these psychologically disturbed people who looked so normal, and we very much wondered what upsetting things had happened in their early lives to produce such violent opposition to direct commands and requests, such disinclination to face people. He went on to say that their job, as they saw it, was to get the children taught somehow, and his instructions to his staff were that when they felt resistance beginning in a boy they were to alter their tactics immediately and try to get at the problem they were teaching from a different angle. They were in fact practising 'avoiding' tactics, which in the circumstances seemed wholly justified. They had forty-four severe problems all needing some passes at 'O' level and they achieved some commendable successes with these.

It seemed to us a most alarming training for life, as we could not imagine any walk of work where one could hope to avoid a direct order from somebody at some stage, and it did not seem that these boys with all this cushioning were being prepared for the hard world. However, this school was perhaps concentrating on the one job of getting the necessary exams passed, and if these tactics were being successful then maybe the consequent confidence gained by the successful boys was the necessary strengthener for the next stage.

Whatever and however that may have been, these avoiding tactics were the very worst thing for Freddy and when the headmaster so reasonably agreed with us on this, we were just bewildered and disappointed that saying so had not come from him. I expect he would happily have let Freddy laze along getting nowhere until he had to leave through old age.

It was difficult to discover if he had any feelings of urgency or misgiving about the actual future of any of his boys. We did feel that he was so engrossed in his endless search to find ways and means of reaching the resisting, that he had lost sight of the ultimate goal which we thought was to educate people to live in the world.

When my husband finally tackled him again on the delicate subject of his school being registered but not recognized, he told us a very brave and rather gallant thing.

When, at his frequent request, schools inspectors came, they always handed him a printed form consisting of headings for the various types of school that one can run, asking him which his was. He said that on each occasion he put his pen through the lot and wrote in, at the bottom, his own heading which was 'school for the educationally inhibited'. Nothing more was ever heard of this but he said he was going to continue to hit this nail on its head until it finally began to go in, as he believed fervently that there were children fitting precisely this description, unrecognized and needing as much help as any others.

The cynics can laugh but, futile as his policy was for Freddy, I am sure it was a life-saver for many ultra-sensitive boys and we expressed a sincere hope that one day through his perseverance this condition would be formally recognized.

I enquired about art and drama, but he successfully avoided replying. We came away with no ideas what to do for the best for Freddy.

12

We ascended the stairs in stockinged feet. They were narrow, steep stairs and covered in blue carpet. They belonged to a ski-jumping champion and his wife. We had rented a room in their new chalet and we left our boots in their hall.

The holidays spent while Freddy was at the Sussex school had taken on a new character. Our family was gently disintegrating as Jean and Heather grew on and lived more independently from us, and there we were only three of us, my husband, Freddy and I, skiing together in France.

Freddy shared our room in true French fashion; he slept on a truckle bed at the foot of ours. There was a telly squeezed into what space was left and one Sunday evening I decided to practise my French and try to follow a film. It was an old Deanna Durbin and it was dubbed. Freddy joined me—there was plenty of room for him to curl up beside me on our outsize bed without disturbing my husband who was also there, but reading a book.

The plot was unravelling itself between bouts of soggy song but I was in a hopeless muddle. 'Oh, *what* did he say?' I cried. To my consternation Freddy replied that 'the Manager in the night-club had got it'. I turned round sharply and looked at him. My husband put down his book. Freddy, of course, was lip-reading American!

Freddy was a reckless and rather messy skier. We understood the attraction he found in speed and dash, but to counteract the lackadaisical time he was spending at school we tried to make him concentrate on style. He knew the basic principles but applying these was a different matter and required effort and trouble he was not always prepared to make or take. He often resented our criticisms partly because he knew them to be justified and I hoped he was learning that there was no short cut to good skiing or living.

He ended up in a blaze of triumph. The previous year Heather had broken all records by using sixty tickets' worth of ski-lifts in one day. Freddy woke up one morning and said 'Mum, I'm going to beat Heather, are you?' 'I'll try' I answered, and we set off. We had bought abonnements at the beginning of the holiday but we knew what each lift was worth and we added up the ticket values as we went.

By 5.15 pm I was defeated at fifty-eight. I knew that had my life depended upon it, I could not have tackled one more ski-run.

I sent Freddy off up a lift worth three tickets and floundered back to the car with shaking knees and aching legs. 'Done it!' he exclaimed when he joined us and we congratulated him and hoped Heather would not mind too much and I rejoiced inwardly because I felt this spirit in Freddy to be up and doing, to respond to challenge and to assert himself bode well for the future.

Skiing lasted only two weeks in the year and during the rest of the school holidays we tried to arrange and encourage constructive activities which would help Freddy to feel he was secure in and belonged to the world around him. We were delaying, postponing, avoiding—I do not know which—confronting ourselves about the future. It remained there, poker-faced, and we continued helplessly uninspired. But Freddy loved the forest we lived near and local gossip had it that the head gamekeeper there was a good man and a great 'character'.

We went to the forest one summer evening. It was a dreaming place. We were surrounded by the warmth of summer and willowherb. Time stood still. Mr Teller lived in an 'estate' cottage and his garden looked like the cover of a catalogue with neat rows of beans, both runner and broad, succulent lettuces and fuzzy carrot tops.

Mrs Teller grew canterbury bells, phlox and sweet williams and her dahlias were as big as sunflowers and she had fruitful blackcurrant bushes. Mr Teller yarned on and on in the gathering evening. We had found him in his gumboots and worn tweed jacket, carrying buckets to the pheasant pens. His blue eyes had twinkling creases at the sides and bushy brows rose and gathered with the enthusiasm he put into everything he said. He had a soft west country voice and watching his ruddy face, which radiated much kindness and good sense, was so pleasurable that I did not listen to his words.

I did catch at intervals in my enjoyment 'fowl pest', 'vermin', or 'caught for six on the off leg' and then he was away on a tirade against the Forestry Commission 'plantin' them little Christmas trees everywhere around when they should be replacin' my oaks and beeches proper like see.' He had asked his MP about it, but he apparently 'didn't seem no good no how about it and what can you do for they say them fir trees pays, but our forest trees, well, there'll be none of them left soon.'

We asked him if he could find jobs for Freddy if he came up during his holidays and we explained briefly about his deafness and his communication problem.

Like most people working close to nature, Mr Teller did not live and work by theories but by wisdom which seemed gathered from nature's rhythm and the weather. He listened to us and he said: 'Well now, that's hard lines on a boy, but he can come up here any time and that'll be grand, there's plenty for a lad to do and we'll see how he gets on see? He may well like it, mending pens and that.' He was totally accepting without being unaware.

And so Freddy padded round the forest with Mr Teller. He saw what a year's work consisted of in pheasant rearing and at the end of it he said 'I love being in the forest, Mum, but the birds are boring.' I was affronted. I always react with unreasonable impatience when the young say they are bored by anything. The word, for me, symbolized the arrogance of youth and I did not like it.

'If you are bored, it's your own fault' I snapped, remembering the resentment and misgivings with which I had received the same statement from my own mother when I was young. But I recalled those little brown birds pecking around in their dusty pens, the scattered feathers, the fuss about water troughs and wire, the smell, the courtly kings they grew into—and it all ending in one colossal blow-up with rows of them dead and delicious. I remembered Mr Teller admitting that 1 October was not his favourite day in the year as he got 'attached to them some'ow see,' and I could not mind that Freddy was not dedicating himself to gamekeeping though it would have been convenient.

In spare moments he hired a horse and rode in the forest and he made friends with a retired general and his family who kept two horses and sometimes needed Freddy to do odd jobs. Like Mr Teller, they understood Freddy in the best possible way. Their words were helpful but their actions spoke louder. One of them would telephone: 'Could Freddy possibly come up for a couple of hours this afternoon?' and he would pedal the four miles to their home. Sometimes he groomed and mucked out the horses and cleaned the tack, and at other times he mowed their lawns or chopped wood, working hard and carefully, and often a mug of tea was passed through the kitchen window or he was pulled in for a pint of beer at the end of the task, which he would drink in the drawing room in his stockinged feet, sitting on the edge of a chair.

On other days there would be neither tea nor beer and this was good. Freddy was learning to take things as they came.

He had noticed workmen leaning on shovels smoking or brewing tea in cosy little canvas caves rigged up on their jobs. He returned home from his first assignment with the General saying 'I *did* work Mum, and no stopping for cigarettes.' They had paid him a nominal sum and both parties had kept a healthy eye on the time put in. His reference to the cigarettes was entirely symbolical as he did not smoke, and though we did he had never shown the slightest inclination to begin. We were thankful, and I had a suspicion that Freddy was too keen on cash to have it go up in smoke which was a perfect deterrent, as the rule in our family was that no one smoked until they were earning their own money, after which it was their own affair. And Freddy was earning.

We had friends he stayed with who knew just how to spoil growing boys. They treated him as an equal and extended his confidence with their kindness and caring. His returns from these sophisticated weekends were complicated by detailed instructions and tips having to be given to disbelieving coach drivers in order to ensure correct changes of buses in Salisbury.

They would look at Freddy and wonder what the fuss was about and it was impossible to explain so we all pretended he was much deafer than he really was and somehow managed to travel and arrive. He revelled in these visits and loved the friends but his thank you letters were a most laborious effort and often had to be rewritten several times.

And during another holiday we discovered Lundy Island and spent three days there in a hired cottage in a heatwave. Freddy was touched by the magic of being surrounded by sea, cliffs, bracken and birds.

And there were always visits to 'Grandpa's farm' and reunions with Jack.

To many it must have seemed that Freddy had a great life

and certainly he responded warmly and appreciatively to all the expeditions we organized and the experiences we put in his way, but in spite of his enthusiasm, his gaiety and his enquiring mind and because of his handicaps, as he struck fifteen a huge hazard hung over it all. It was social, and it was about friends.

For these he relied entirely on ourselves. There was a boy living near us, who was the younger son in a family of two boys and a girl. A certain degree of friendship sprang up between Freddy and Patrick but our neighbour had it all his own way. This child called for Freddy if he needed him, had nothing better to do or felt in the mood. It was humiliating and disappointing but it was easy to see why.

Like so many of Freddy's relations and acquaintances Patrick, though two years younger than he, commanded a first-class vocabulary, and enjoyed the sophisticated contact with his older brother who brought the current teenage and university jargon into his home. He simply had not the patience required for sustained communication with Freddy, whose skiing and camping experiences and mysterious life in the forest somehow failed to impress Patrick, whereas Freddy was hugely impressed by everything about him. When things went well they had really good times together, out on their bicycles or making dens or playing Monopoly if it rained.

Freddy chose to have 'friends' to supper for a birthday treat. Patrick came, a boy from the local scout troop and another lad well known to the others and slightly to Freddy.

After the supper we had a few games and, once again, Kim's. The things on the tray were the usual haphazard choice. This time I did not have to make allowances for Freddy and he could also do his own writing. I waited to see the results. It was a repetition of that other birthday—Freddy had them all out cold with a score of eighteen to their twelves and thirteens. This was good, as he had been hopelessly left out of the supper-time conversation which had centred round some film they had all seen.

'Do you remember that bit when . . .' Patrick was off.

'Oh yes and when the car went over the cliff,' interrupted the boy scout.

'And wasn't it funny when the policeman . . .' the others carried on. Then they all talked at once and began to shout out their varying reactions. I watched Freddy. His face was alight and he wore a desperately eager expression, wanting to be of and with the others. They spoke too quickly, they darted from one action to another as they remembered the more dramatic scenes and Freddy could neither follow nor relate their descriptions to what he remembered himself.

Listening to Freddy describing any film he had seen was something for which I do not believe the most saintly of saints could have found patience. Very few children can achieve coherence when doing this, but it was a shattering experience discovering that Freddy had missed most of the main points, failed to gather who was bad or good, or why, and was generally as muddled as ten pounds of wool lost in a drawer for five years with moths.

As Freddy struggled with the film at his birthday supper, getting the wrong sense, the wrong meaning and the wrong man, it became clear that only our presence at the table was restraining these lads from heaving exaggerated sighs, rolling their eyes heavenwards as if asking for patience and strength or saying to Freddy '*Do* you mind?'

No blame on the boys. One cannot expect children of twelve and thirteen to have patience or sensitivity and we never did. It is jungle law at that stage and all the horrors of *The Lord of the Flies* became to me extremely relevant and far too real.

Freddy's situation emphasized the terrible vulnerability of the weaker when trying to survive. Nevertheless in certain ways he developed from these encounters. He was becoming more and more aware that he was at a disadvantage but he was not going under or turning in on himself. He was developing determination, and without any thickening of his skin was nevertheless quite forcefully imposing himself on society.

Freddy was gregarious and he enjoyed people and seemed to have a very marked and strong instinct for survival where making social contacts were concerned. He said a very nice 'thank you' to us for his birthday treat after seeing his guests off the premises. He was aware that the party for him had left something to be desired and had not gone with all the zip and zest it might have, but he had enjoyed the formality and the seriousness with which we had treated the occasion.

'Very Wembley,' I said to Jean on the telephone when she rang next day and asked how Freddy's party had gone. This was a phrase we used among ourselves to indicate the measure of Freddy's situations; of course it came from the old joke about the two deaf men speaking to each other.

'Is this Wembley?' asks one.

'No, it's Thursday' says the other.

'Yes so am I, let's go and have one' says the first, and it was all too much of a daily occurrence in our household for it to be in any way funny any more.

A sort of hangover of concern hovered for days after the party. A restive mood settled on me and inwardly I wittered about the elusive thing Freddy lacked, which would have made such a fantastic difference to him and his life had it been there.

His relationship with Patrick continued the same way—Freddy the stoodge, Freddy who ran to the other's bidding at the drop of a hat, Freddy with dashed hopes, Freddy invited over for a bare hour and made so happy. We did not like the imbalance, particularly as there were sometimes patronizing attitudes.

Some time after the birthday party Patrick made an arrangement to meet Freddy at 2.30 one Sunday afternoon for something rather special. Freddy was ready and waiting but Patrick never came. He broke the engagement to go out somewhere with his brother. We had a long talk to Freddy about this. It was something he himself would not have done to anyone and certainly not without at least leaving a note. So we told him that he had got to stand up for himself and demand an explanation.

Freddy did not want to do this and began to think up reasons, many of them, as to why things had possibly and probably gone wrong. We kept to our point, explaining that although all his excuses for Patrick were reasonable, he could still have let Freddy know and that it was no way to behave. We also tried to help him to understand that there was a lack of dignity in allowing yourself to become somebody's door-mat and that the only hope for a good sound friendship was one based upon mutual respect.

He marched over the road and had his say. Patrick was covered in guilty confusion. He apologized sincerely and profusely and they now enjoy a very pleasant regard for one another. Freddy took a good leap forward when he overcame his initial cowardice and forced himself to make his stand; it cleared the air and after that he was freer, more relaxed and somehow taller.

13

We needed no convincing that Freddy had the capacity to learn more. We were determined to find some way of stretching him to his academic limits. I was more and more conscious of the other thousands of children in Britain with handicaps like Freddy and I kept wondering about them. I was appalled and haunted by the thought that if we had not had the means with which to get some more education for Freddy, he would be in the world by now and having to make a go of it and earn his own living. He was not ready for this in any way and the thought of any child in the same state at this stage and age working a man's day struck me as grossly inhumane.

We wrote to Millfield again, reminding them that we had written four years previously, explained that Freddy could now cope without specialized teachers of the deaf, and asked if there was the faintest hope of their having him for just one year, to get some first-class games and acquire some further basic schooling with their renowned reputation for a serious attitude to scholarship.

Once again the headmaster replied with great sympathy saying he did not see how or where he could fit him into their curriculum and that anyway there was not so much as broom cupboard space left in the school.

In fairness to him we had enclosed copies of Freddy's latest letters, and when we thought about them and Millfield together, well yes, where indeed could he be fitted in? But it had been worth trying because that headmaster was the kind of man who would have found a way for a child had it been humanly possible.

My husband and I were in close proximity in a telephone box outside Chelmsford GPO. Someone had traced obscure patterns with a fat finger across the dusty squares of window and we were stepping on cigarette ends and discarded bus tickets.

We were there because it wasn't fair to talk French over

Freddy's head and we couldn't possibly talk about him in front
of him. He was in our car, parked under a lime tree down the
street and we were trying to make up our minds about his life.
We were also trying to telephone someone who knew someone
else whom we wanted to know about.

We got through but our friend had to be fetched from the
garden and by the time he was speaking to us, breathless from
his lawn mower, we were out of small change and the line had
gone dead. Once again we were having to make a decision
and, as always with Freddy, there wasn't any proper choice.

Since we had spoken to the headmaster at the Sussex school
and since he had not suggested that he changed his tactics with
Freddy, it seemed obvious that wherever else he go, he should
leave them. We had spent all the summer holidays not knowing
what to do until, after the rejection from Millfield, I had seen
an article in a magazine describing a family living in an old
priory in Lincolnshire. The mother was a graduate and ran
a tutorial establishment. I had written to her, enclosing Gillian
Freeman's *New Statesman* piece which I felt explained our
situation better than a lengthy letter from me and adding that
the highly recommended school in Sussex was not being
effective.

I had approached Freddy very gently on the subject of
leaving Sussex.

'How do you feel about your school?' I had asked.

'I like it' he had said, 'and I like the people even though
Mr S is rather funny and I'm rather cross about no history.'

'I know you like them' I had said, 'but do you think you
are spelling any better or learning sums?'

There had been a thoughtful pause and then a reluctantly
honest reply. 'Well, not really I suppose.'

I then told him about Lincolnshire and showed him the
magazine article. 'I've written to them' I said, 'and they've
suggested we go over to see them and spend the night there
before you go back to school. What do you think? We think
it might be better than Sussex but of course we must all go
and see first.'

'Will there be hockey?' he asked and I replied that that was
exactly the kind of thing we hoped to discover and he must
ask the people such questions himself.

We were much relieved that the thought of the possibility of leaving Sussex was not the great blow for him we had expected. I had been dreading even broaching the mere suggestion, and later that day I asked him if he could tell me what he would feel if he *did* leave and was amazed to hear him say, 'I don't really mind and if I learn better at the new place perhaps I'll get some exams.' Exams was a word which was beginning to have an ever greater meaning in our household. Since the wonderful day when Heather achieved three 'A' levels, two with A grades, there had been talk of exams at regular intervals. Jean was getting on steadily with her nursing career and the inevitable exams concerning that kept cropping up and Heather was constantly sitting exams with her university course. Cousins were taking 'O' and 'A' levels and getting, or failing to get places at universities or technical colleges. Patrick had won a choral scholarship to a cathedral school so of course he had taken exams. I looked at Freddy and knew that examwise he was a non-starter and I wondered just how much this was going to matter to him because I was convinced that in his heart of hearts, he knew too. How much did he *mind*? It wasn't the moment to expound our theory and belief that exams are not everything. If Freddy had aspirations then exams could act as a self-induced dangling carrot as well as anything else, so we left the matter there.

We had arrived in Lincolnshire on a dank, dripping September evening.

Often if Freddy was sitting in the back of the car, I would find a face coming round over my left shoulder trying to see my mouth for the vital lip-reading. This journey my husband was at the wheel and I was beside him. Freddy, from the back, suddenly said 'Oh please look at me, Mum. I can't see what you're saying.' The phrase struck us forcefully and was so perfectly explicit of the extra effort required of people with physical handicaps. It arrested our thoughts and helped us to understand a bit more how much of a tax on the patience of such people these small irritations must be. I marvelled again that Freddy was as good-natured as he was under these circumstances.

The old priory loomed up from its shroud of yew and other evergreens. We pulled the bell-pull and heard a jangle echoing hollowly through the building.

Suddenly the door opened and our hostess introduced herself and welcomed us in. It was about 8.30 in the evening and after coffee Freddy was banished to a frugal cell for the night and we got down to our talking.

Once again we tried to explain the painful problems of learning which were exclusive to Freddy. I left most of the talking to my husband but I do remember at one point bursting out with passion, that no one seemed to understand that people could be both backward and intelligent. Mrs L's husband had joined us and was helpful in the discourse. We talked until after midnight. My husband repeatedly pointed out that we felt the most vital need was to see that Freddy had his mind exercised and taxed but at the same time his spirit encouraged.

We warned them that he had been idle for too long, that he was as human as everyone else and did not take kindly to real brain slog but that we felt there must be one final effort made before his schooling was over.

We got in first by asking them not to ask us what we thought he was going to do in life. That, we stressed, could come later if we sent him to learn with them. I did state, however, that he had done some regular work with a gamekeeper during his holidays and he had seen the season round.

We also warned them that they would at first think all was plain sailing then begin to discover the yawning gaps, the deficiencies and the vast expanses of blank non-comprehension. They told us that speech therapy could be arranged at the local hospital and this was good news indeed.

They also said there was a youth club nearby which we felt would help fill in the gap made by leaving a school full of boys. Riding was available with a retired brigadier, they were keen that he do arts and crafts, he was apparently going to be able to join in both hockey and rugby football with the local school, and it looked as if Freddy, if he went there, was never going to have a split second free from activity.

They said they did not yet know who the other children were going to be the following term, but probably a French girl or two and possibly a German boy.

We went to our room, next to Freddy's, down a creaking corridor. It was frugally bare, but comfortable. It looked out onto the roof of a yellow stucco stable block with a wooden clock tower and the yews and evergreens could be seen beyond the old slate roofs. Next day we descended a sloping staircase to an enormous kitchen. It was homely and an Aga burned a warm morning welcome and there was a dog basket and pegs on the wall for coats for very small people. This had been the priory refectory, the stone tiles gleamed and a large brass chandelier hung from the ceiling giving the room the air of a Dutch interior. After breakfast Freddy disappeared with Mrs L while one of her sons showed us round.

Mrs L said that if it helped us to make up *our* minds, she could tell us that after sleeping on it and thinking some more and talking to Freddy, she would be willing to take him the term after Christmas. We thanked her and left. And that is how we came to be in the telephone box, which was becoming stuffy beyond endurance and where nothing was being solved.

We were having intense thoughts about the Priory and some doubts. We were not convinced that the 'Ls' really had a grip on Freddy's situation or that, if and when they discovered it, they would treat it with the deep sympathy and understanding and encouragement it required. One thing was certain: we were confirmed in our belief in the rightness that whatever else was to happen, the coming term was to be his last in Sussex. We felt strongly that Freddy had got to start some real growing up and the life going on at the Priory was a great deal more adult and sophisticated than the Sussex haven of inconsequentiality.

That determined, we felt better and my husband signed the letter he had typed before leaving home, giving a term's notice for Freddy to leave the Sussex school. We drove on to Sussex, explaining to Freddy that we had not yet decided about Lincolnshire but that we *had* decided about Sussex. He was happy with these arrangements and enthused about a possible life there more than we did. We promised to let him know what we decided on the instant and as it was unreasonable to keep him in suspense, we would be compelled to come to some decision.

It was six o'clock in the evening when we reached the school and after depositing Freddy and his trunk and bicycle with strong talk about making yet another 'last term' a good one, we left.

Heather was waiting when we got in and wanted to know everything about our trip. She, like us, said that whatever else, he must leave Sussex. We told her our conclusions had been the same. We then spent four days discussing the Priory. We were still uncertain but the awful question was: if not there, then where? There was no real choice. There never had been with Freddy. It was us choosing to go on and on trying to find something, somewhere, better, that landed us with alternatives. And this required nerve-cracking decisions based almost solely on intuition. We had no other guide.

It was the speech therapy which clinched the deal. The promise of regular speech therapy was so good that we wrote to Mrs L and formally asked her to take Freddy in January. At the end of that Christmas term we went to fetch him and his belongings from Sussex. He had made attachments during the two years spent there and there were things he was going to miss. The headmaster's wife was pretty and he kissed her goodbye when we left.

14

Schooling in Lincolnshire left a lot to be desired. Freddy experienced the shock of discovering that to be lonely when surrounded by people is the ultimate in loneliness.

He was never really happy at this school and at one stage positively belligerent. None of the good things promised quite came off. The brigadier's riding had proved monotonous, unimaginative and very expensive so he ceased attending. Ventures to the local youth club were equally unsuccessful but whether because of Freddy's acute discomfort and embarrassment when trying to communicate with people, particularly his contemporaries, or because none of the rest of the family went with him or because he just did not like it when he got there, we never quite found out. The rugger suggested never happened at all; hockey disappeared in the January mud of that year and was never heard of again.

I had met the speech therapist and found her warm, experienced and very kind. However, Freddy was still failing to pronounce 'ing' and word endings, and words like max, six, sticks etc. all ended in a messy kind of lisp. I begged Mrs L to correct these faults whenever they occurred but always felt my suggestions were received with slight irritation. I wondered why. During the second term I really talked about it at length, as we were finding Freddy's speaking almost unbearably bad and could see endless and possibly insurmountable social problems for him over this in the future. Eventually Mrs L spoke to the speech therapist and the verdict came back that if one insisted too strongly the child might stop speaking altogether.

For some children that may have been so, and I could see this as a very real possibility at a more tender age, but not our Freddy at sixteen-and-a-half, and my heart sank to think that they had discovered so little about him—had not got the measure of him at all. There was excuse enough for the therapist, as she could not get to know him in the half-hour allotted to her each week, but Mrs L had him in her life all and every day and must have known there was small likelihood of such an occurrence.

We thought we had made it clear that insistent effort on all fronts was what we were after. The smallest child in the family went to the local school daily and Freddy developed a bond of a sort with her. Mrs L expressed concern and some irritation again that Freddy seemed happy to play childish games and get up to dam-making and house-building projects with this child at weekends. If she felt this was too childish, we wondered why she didn't suggest, and if necessary insist on, more adult activities.

Freddy had collected some futile jokes from the school in Sussex which we termed 'Freddy's wet jokes' and which we gently discouraged as they were embarrassing in their inanity. They were, however, a sheet anchor for him at this stage. He desperately needed to feel 'of the party' and as meal-time conversation was one of the things he found most difficult, when he felt left out and overtaken beyond endurance, he would come out hopelessly irrelevantly with some of his 'wet' jokes. Two of them went thus. Question: 'Why do cows have bells?' Answer: 'Because their horns don't work.' And then the story of the football goalkeeper who let ball after ball through the posts and when asked by the captain 'Why?', replied 'What is the net for?' And in this vein there were several more.

There was always some kind person who laughed, and sometimes we all laughed and he would feel partially successful though always sensitive to the situation and in full knowledge that he was pushing himself. We very much wanted this phase to pass and as we hoped it was just a question of time we groaned inwardly and let the jokes go without comment.

Mrs L complained about these jokes which Freddy had apparently inflicted upon her family not once but several times.

We looked at her in astonishment and suggested if she thought them poor and that he should be growing out of them, then to say so to him, for it was for precisely this that we had sent him to her. We felt more and more that not only did she not understand, but she was bored by it all. But Freddy learnt some elementary typewriting and a nice old man gave him painting lessons which he loved; he made me a thonged leather purse; he increased his general knowledge from the television current affairs programmes; he cycled about in Lincolnshire and grew interested in the flat countryside and he learnt a lot about people. He developed a bond with a pretty French girl and stood up to and answered, sometimes with scorn, a twenty-five-year-old German who stayed in bed late and fussed about going outside if it was so much as drizzling with rain. But there was a yellow dog which he often had to exercise and which he just could not like and he was always cold, both outside and in, cold because there was not enough love or fun around—love of the kind that keeps out the cold. One of his letters read thus:

Dear Mum and Dad.

Thank you for your letters and I am very well. My work is all right and it all well, but I do feel that next time I do typing on Thursday I would feel like running away because it is not very good and cancel it for it is a bit difficult to explain here.

The weather has been like the days we had on Lundy. It is a bit cloudy today but I hope it would clear up later.

I had not been playing hockey since I told you about it when I first played, and no more because of the weather and so mony of the matches had been missed.

My money box is allright but I have gone to for behind to catch up. And I do like the new stamp.

You knows the German boy well he throught that he could take me down and stay for a night or two to exspolor the country side for he had been studing our area from an evening class. I am not sure what date yet unless you think this is a good idea if the ansewer yes I will tell you what our plan for the day on arrivall if it is not it would have to be cancell and dad would have to come up to take me home.

I do go up to the yourth club on Tuesdays according to what has to be done first, ie prep, or to look after the children if no one is in the house.

I must stop now, it time for lunch 1.15? or 1.30 so I will
replie about going home when I have the answer from you.

Best love Freddy

During the time with the Ls one of them said: 'You know
you are wrong about Freddy being intelligent but backward.
It is not possible. Consider the derivation of the word
intelligent. It comes from intellect. Freddy has not got intellect.'
This bald statement hit me between the eyes. I had evolved the
phrase after months of puzzling out how it was that Freddy
was backward yet so often so quick and so bright. I had always
used it in discussions on the subject as the clearest way to
illustrate his situation and I felt it had been encouragement
to others I met who had similar problems.

It had become a fixed idea with me, and I had to take a
deep breath and try to open my mind.

'Well then' I said rather crossly, 'common sense.'

'Yes' replied Mr L, 'lots of it, but do forget about the
intelligence. He can't do maths and he can't think theoretically
or grasp concepts or appreciate thought process, etc.'

Mr L had made a sweeping statement. I knew I had got to
do some re-thinking. I think he was justified in using these
undefined terms in this context, as they referred exclusively
to Freddy's brain power. I spent weeks after that thinking
about intellectuality and common sense.

I felt that at the moment when Mr L made his pronounce-
ment, in their minds they virtually wrote Freddy off. After
that they went through the motions of helping him but I don't
think they were truly interested.

Lacking in intellect Freddy may have been, but he
appreciated things of the mind and I knew this was one of the
secrets of living. He was at a disadvantage living in a world of
thinking people who mostly read extensively and indulged in
a lot of mildly serious talking. He had grown to like this
society even if he could not compete with it on equal terms,
and it added extra complexity to his problems.

I once said to my husband that it seemed we had done a
terrible thing, bringing Freddy up to enjoy and appreciate a
way of life with which he was not able to cope. What else
could we have done? We too had to survive and the only way

we knew was by being ourselves. We tried to reassure ourselves by believing that it must be good and in some ways valuable, the extent to which Freddy enjoyed his surroundings, but we were very concerned about his own awareness of his limitations at this time, and always afraid we could have done better for him.

Another letter read:

Dear Mum and Dad,

How are you. I hope that you both arrived home saftly. I have settled down now and enjoying myself. Please let me know when it is grandmor's birthday for I have compleatly forgotten the date.

I have not got very much to say exsept thank you both very much for a marvoules holiday and London including lundy.

Dad going back to modles trains, Mrs L says that she has got a guid after a trin epolishiin when she took Ken, soying that she sow the modle of the liyiling railway of the one in walks. If I have the peco oo, 9 I could work to my plain as it was before. In the promplit it has the pictures of the qurrey men and the small locomotives. I'll be glad if we could work or solve money for that bisness.

In my bedroom cubord, their is my cash box with a money guid of the value. Could you find out what the worth is of a 1901 penny the year Queen Victoria died.

The trees here are beutifell green chestnut trees that produst conytersts!!!

I hope that you have discovered that your bike is in the shop for repair which by now is finnished. Sorry to make you angry if you did not know what had happened to it. I was ment to tell you but I had forgotten.

I'ved played tennis the other day and it was not bod. But I thourght that the French girls could play very well, but it turned out to be begginers. All over agoin for me! never mind it had to be done.

The weather has been a bit dull. rain mot anough sun but lost of heavy and aight clouds. The heavy clouds are a leverl the come over slowly and produce noide. The light clouds come in to mony long numbers and cover the sun.

Best love, Freddy

136

The sun was dancing brilliantly on the little waves and they were sparkling back; the warm smell of hamburgers wafted greasily over us as we sat on the decks with our tents and baggage and seven hundred other people. We were going to Lundy again, Lundy that was paradise to Freddy and me, elemental Island where time was measured in terms of winds and tides. Unlike the day trippers we were landing for two weeks. Freddy and I were being employed.

We were going to camp in the compound of the old lighthouse and cook for deep sea divers. Much too near to us a fat boy sicked up pink lemonade with his chips and several older people were seen threatened and hurrying towards the cloak-room, but nothing could spoil things for us.

This was one of the very few times that Freddy was really happy while he was sixteen. When he was quite small and we all suffered extremes of despair over trying to live successfully with his condition, I remember knowing even then that the worst time for Freddy was still to come, that as awareness grew and self-realization, he would wake to the fact of his inadequacies. And the time was now.

Lundy loomed, rather bare, her sheer cliff faces shimmering in the afternoon sunshine. Gulls swirled and cawed in and around the granite ruins of the once substantial buildings on top of the cliffs. The Trinity House Lighthouse sat secure at the south end of the island in its gleaming white, newly-painted security, surrounded by busy important little buildings, a cable house, engine-rooms.

Suddenly figures appeared, moving about the island. We could distinguish the road snaking its way down to the landing beach and people running down it to meet our ship. The old slipway was alive with the colour and activity of our divers. They had their hut there and were flashing about in their rubber dinghies with the outboard motors.

Six hundred and eighty-eight people had been lowered into three large open boats manned by veritable pirates who all seemed to have golden hair and beards. Everything about these men spelled glamour—their faded blue jeans, their waders and their torn shirts or bare sunburned torsos, but above all their beards! We fell from the deck into their iron arms and the open boats, and our bags were thrown after us.

137

A quick turn around of the launch, and more pirates were lifting us out onto the mobile landing stage with its rusty wheels, and then we set off down a plank walk with a detachable hand rail and finally stepped down onto the stony beach.

We took care avoiding the wire ropes and the winch stretching up the beach to a waiting tractor which revved and plunged and pulled like a bronco as the tide came in and the landing stage with it.

We made our way to our new home in the compound of the old lighthouse and brewed tea in the tiny kitchen while waiting for the tractor to dump our belongings. By evening our tents were pitched and we had met Tony and Bill and two Johns, who were instructing the divers on a course in Deep Sea Diving.

Next morning the outgoing cook left and we took over. In the tiny kitchen there was a tiny calor-gas stove. It had three rings, a grill and an oven. Through the dining room and at the back of the lighthouse-keeper's house was the scullery with the pump for the water and a calor-gas boiler for heating water for washing, washing clothes and washing up. We varied in number from eleven to seventeen, as people came and went on the courses, and everyone needed a good cooked breakfast, a packed lunch and a three-course evening meal.

Freddy's routine was soon established. He got up early and set the great table. He then climbed over the north wall of the compound and gathered mushrooms for everyone's breakfast. His final job was making the toast. I couldn't have managed without him. After that he was free until 7 pm when he set the table for supper, served the soup and cleared the dishes.

He would go down to the divers' beach and make himself indispensable fetching and carrying, filling air cylinders, clearing out the hut, baling the rubber dinghies. He also found time to pay social calls on the islanders and he was invariably plied with homemade cakes when he called on the Agent's wife. One day he spent with the farmer loading lambs into the Lundy Gannet to be taken to Bideford for the sales. We spent one or two evenings in the tavern when acquaintance was renewed with the Austrian barmen, islanders and the lighthouse men.

Freddy was wary of them. He had been more guarded and

less trusting with strangers since an encounter with a Trinity House maintenance engineer the previous spring.

We had rented Castle Cottage for a week in the Easter holidays and had gone there with the prospect of path-clearing and bramble-pulling. We had taken Petr with us. Petr was a Czechoslovak student who had been on holiday in England when the crisis came in 1968 and had decided to stay. His vocabulary at that time had consisted of Yes, No, Please, Thank you, *all* the titles and words of *all* the Beatles' records— and Beer. He was struggling with 'A' level work, physics and maths, as he had gained a place at an English university provided he succeeded in these exams. We had room in our house and in our hearts for him as he wrestled with his conscience and convictions in a situation quite outside any experience of ours.

Freddy liked Petr and a happy relationship established itself between these two. It had the flavour of the trenches, a spirit of sharing, of tolerance, trust and loyalty. It was relaxed and uncritical. Petr borrowed Freddy's toothpaste and Freddy Petr's comb.

I was trying to encourage Freddy with further understanding of word-meanings and better speech articulation and at the same time I was helping Petr with language in general. Freddy sometimes found that he could put Petr right on words and this was good for his confidence and morale, both of which were at a particularly low ebb. We had been discussing his future as we hacked at the encroaching gorse along the pathway to the hotel. Not being happy in Lincolnshire made him gloomy and dissatisfied. His manners had deteriorated and echoed the time when he had been in the class for backward children at our local school. He had failed to open the tavern door for one of the islanders the previous evening. Her arms had been filled with cardboard boxes and he had just stood by and let her struggle. I reminded him of this, explaining that it really wasn't good enough, and he asked in a tone of irate petulance 'Why *do* men have to open doors for ladies anyway?'

'Because' I replied firmly, 'the ladies have the babies!'

Freddy had thought deeply for a long moment and decided to settle for opening doors—definitely.

But he wasn't definite about his future. Not at all. Perversely, he listed all the things for which he knew he could not be considered on account of his deafness. The army, the police force, a pilot. In this state of dejection he was falling back on his old loves in the *security* of their *impossibility*. Freddy was rarely sorry for himself but he suddenly looked at me and, near to tears, declared 'I'm no *good* and I'll have to have a wife and some children and I'll want a car.' This was a shock. I had no idea that Freddy was so conscious of the basic facts about earning, but I welcomed his realism.

And then in the tavern he had been truly taken for a ride. We had had dinner in the hotel and stayed on by the fire talking to people. Petr had borrowed a guitar from a young artist and was playing Czech folk songs in a corner. Freddy found himself at the bar with the Trinity House man, being bought pints of shandy and given the whole life-cycle of maintenance engineers.

About 11.30 pm I told the boys to come home together and I left the cheerful warmth of the tavern for my bed, book and candles. The muffled munch and low breathing of the sheep guided me to the stone wall in whose shadow they huddled, the lights of the sheltering ships twinkled and bobbed as they too huddled together in the bay.

Freddy was very excited and slightly flushed when he and Petr returned. He had lost count of the number of shandies he had put away, he had a date with the maintenance man to go round the South Lighthouse next morning and had been given two hours of opinions on the married 'state' and the role of women in and out of it. He collapsed on his bunk feeling, I think, more relaxed than he had for a long time. He had been accepted in his own right in the world, and the world had been of men.

Freddy was all for another session in the tavern next night. I tried to dissuade him and I wanted to warn him that a repetition of the previous evening was most unlikely, but he was determined. Sure enough, when we called in after dinner, his friend of the domestic philosophy and maintenance routine merely tossed him a friendly nod and took up one of the islanders in conversation.

I could feel Freddy smarting with disappointment and shock,

so after a short stay I caught Petr's eye and we made for home. We all linked arms and marched back to our cottage, swinging and swaying and pretending to knock one another down.

Our cottage was chilly and damp inside but we had some cocoa and card games and made our own good cheer before bedtime. I managed to explain the situation to Petr and it was not difficult as he had noticed almost all of it himself and registered everything in the most sensitive way. He said to me: 'I begin to see how it is with Freddy. When you first told me about him I just could not understand, and I am still thinking I know I could teach hims some maths.'

'Go right ahead' I encouraged, '*do*'. But my tone of voice implied that he would soon find out how mistaken he was.

Freddy had had a bewildering experience. He had been used by that maintenance man for the audience that was so necessary to him. He had talked himself out on Freddy as the gale had blown itself out on the island and next day as the ships left the shelter of the bay, Freddy, after his conducted tour of the lighthouse, was left.

For some time after this he would say at odd intervals 'He was a *nice* man wasn't he?' or 'Well, it was nice of him to show me round the lighthouse, wasn't it?' and 'Do you think he's ever taken anyone else round?' and 'He says wives ought to stay at home and not go out to work.'

Later Petr had had his go with the maths teaching which he tackled with all the enthusiasm of a Czech challenged but to absolutely no effect.

But this time, staying in the old lighthouse, Freddy was quite specially happy. He was very proud of his identity with the island. People soon greeted him with 'Oh yes, you're up at the Old Light aren't you?' This made him feel important and part of the establishment. He did his chores for me well and with zest, and he found it was very nice being paid.

He put everything he'd got into the help he gave others and he looked carefree and very well with his hair blown about and the air of self-possession and rough dignity that was induced by being a vital cog in the island's wheel. He laughed readily, he was alert and he noticed everything, birds, moths, flowers, tiny beetles and, of course, the seals.

One evening there was a fancy dress party arranged. Freddy was very keen to go. I looked round the lighthouse and could only see pan lids and rolls of old oil-stained twine. Nothing daunted, Freddy said it didn't matter. I was busy assembling an earlier than usual meal for my hungry divers and had neither energy nor time to spare for inspiration. And then at 8 pm Freddy stood before me, eyes wildly alight, draped toga-fashion in one of the lighthouse blankets, wearing a head dress of bracken kept in place with twine and wielding a forked stick which he had spent some time peeling and scraping.

'It's terrific' I said. 'What are you?'

'Oh', he replied, 'well, just the island really' and off he went to the party full of excitement and anticipation.

Freddy spent an enchanted evening; no-one recognized his get-up but that did not bother him. He knew what he was and in this knowledge lay his marvellous confidence in himself at the party.

It was 2 am as we trekked across the grassland to our tall granite home, shining like silver in the soft but brilliant light. First he shed his blanket, then his ferns, and after handing the former to me he did a sort of prancing dance all the way home. It got wilder and more imaginative as the moonshine turned his head and by the time we had reached the wall of the compound he had done ten somersaults and was cartwheeling and handstanding and spinning round and making himself dizzy and laughing and laughing and throwing himself at the moon and rolling about on the close-cropped turf or into patches of bracken.

Champagne in Tunisia or moonshine on Lundy Island, exotica was the ambiance necessary to unleash Freddy.

He fell into bed, and into a deep contented sleep, saying before he did so : 'I love this place.'

And so the days passed. The divers dived, we cooked their meals and then it was the end of August and we were needing to light the hurricane lamps in the evenings. I knew I could not cook for many nights more in this murky light, not without running grave risks of putting currants in the soup or black pepper in the custard. We left one beautiful afternoon. Late summer sun blazed upon us as we scrubbed out our little galley and packed up the remaining stores to be collected by the tractor along with our tents and bags.

With beautiful trophies of coral, enormous sea urchins in exquisite shades of orange, purple, red and green, and a magnificent crayfish, all presented by the divers, we made our way to their beach where the dinghies and equipment were safely packed for departure. The season was over and they were shutting up shop. The Campbells steamer lay in the bay and the boatmen were chugging out with the passengers for re-embarkation. Some of them could be seen hurrying down the path.

The propellers of the steamer vibrated and churned, the clank of anchor chains rattled and smashed onto the deck, the ship shook and moved, and we were off. Freddy and I hung with the divers over the rail, straining towards the island we were so loath to leave. Everyone felt desolate, everyone was feverishly making impossible plans for a life there. No one said anything, but at intervals we looked at each other and experienced a warm communion together of shared thoughts and emotions.

Ilfracombe was sighted and instantly we were all overtaken by the rush and bustle of our old lives. Where were our tickets? What time did buses leave to catch trains? When did everyone start work again? It all seemed so trivial and unnecessary.

15

Before going to Lundy to cook, life at home had been hectic. The house had been like the Club Méditerranée with an endless stream of young people staying. A French girl came for a month and I gave her and Petr English lessons every morning. Nieces and nephews came for a dance.

Freddy was excited about this. It was his first. His problems were no less than those confronting any sixteen-year-old boy—with his ever present hazard of mis-hearing and misunderstanding added. We put him through the drill, explaining the form about dancing with each of the girls in turn and making sure they were properly looked after.

We all went to the dance, which was held in an enormous hall. The sound of the band was a deafening killer to conversation and the only possible dance was movement to the beat reverberating through the floor. Freddy was bewildered and disappointed and looked quite defeated. We had to remind him he had chosen to come, that the numbers of people in the party were equalled by his presence and that there was no escape, so he'd better put a smiling face on it and get on as best he could. He was not pleased.

At midnight I had had enough and as other people had joined us and our girls were well attended we decided to give Freddy his reprieve. But a young man had appeared at our table, he and Freddy were deep in a shouting discussion and he did not wish to leave! We were delighted by these developments and, leaving the young to find their own way home, we left to make ourselves a pot of tea and turn down eleven beds.

The sun blazed and we had access to a swimming pool round which we all lay like roasting lizards. We had supper picnics when Petr sat in the long grass playing his folk songs and Beatles' music on his guitar.

An endless stream of young men paid court to the French

girl, Claudette, and I laid the table with extra places for every meal and they were always filled. A godson was making plans to go to a kibbutz on a motor-bike and somebody else was going to Kenya.

Through all this, Freddy frisked like a colt. Between the running dives he performed from the tattered, matted springboard, he absorbed snippets of people's lives, he asked questions, registered the answers firmly in his mind and later took an eager interest in the post-cards which came from every corner of the globe. He revelled in the freedom, the relaxed atmosphere and the stimulation with which we were all injected from everybody's plans. As he was going to do that Lundy cooking he found that he too had plans and was proud and happy to have an equal contribution to make to conversations.

We felt it important that Petr have the chance to earn some money and give himself a break, so we helped him to get work with a firm of civil engineers. And then Freddy set off with his father to walk thirty-six miles of the Ridgeway. They took nothing but a pack between them and as I deposited them at their starting point wearing their khaki shorts and knee-length stockings, they looked for all the world like Empire builders striding out to defeat the natives and stake their claims. Quite suddenly, everyone had gone.

I had the whole day to myself, but I could not settle to anything. I had been too busy for too long to stop abruptly and besides I had too much on my mind. The smouldering question of Freddy's future had been fanned into flames with the forseeable end of Lincolnshire and his seventeenth birthday.

So while he and his father strode across the Downs, I drove to Dorset to see the Franciscan brothers at Cerne Abbas. I was received kindly by a man who had every moment of his life filled with important engagements. He had not really got time to see me at all but he listened patiently while I explained Freddy's state and confided in him our apprehension about his future.

The Brotherhood did a large range of craft activities and also ran a very successful farm, but it was no place for Freddy. The only people they 'took in', so to speak, were people in need of therapy who would stay in their retreat house until they felt better and, of course, any young men joining the Brotherhood.

I felt certain I would collect ideas from there but in fact no seeds were sown at all. I apologized for taking up their precious time and came away in the certainty that we had yet to think in the right way for Freddy.

It was helpful to know what there was that was *not* going to work but at this time there was more crossing off on our list than adding to it.

It was a long journey from Cerne Abbas home, and the house was strangely quiet when I returned in the evening. I climbed the stairs and walked slowly through every room. I was thinking about Petr, his family and the Iron Curtain; Claudette, silly, pretty and spoilt; Graeme, now chugging his way to his kibbutz; Jean with her nursing finals looming and Heather due back from a year spent in Madrid. And then I was in Freddy's room. Freddy with his models and his brass rubbings, his torn Union Jack, a relic from coronation year when he was born and something he probably thought closely connected with *his* Jack. What did it feel like to be Freddy? How did he view his future, from which, as from the dance, there was for him no escape? My mind totally blanked when I got to Freddy, blanked with fear and terrible apprehension for him as the future yawned ahead, hostile in its unpredictability.

My husband and I had been thinking very seriously about this for some time and had done a lot of talking. We wondered if book-binding might appeal and we had consulted one of our closest friends who ran a bookshop. He was very enthusiastic and two days later a book on the subject arrived from him. It was terrifically touching to have anyone react so promptly and practically to our situation and our day was made immeasurably brighter.

Reading it was an impossibility for me, knowing nothing of the trade and being put off by the new terms I should have to memorize, so I perused all the pictures and diagrams and passed it to my husband to digest. He read it all saying it was a very complicated process and he wondered if it was a trade in much demand.

We visited a bookbinder in a big way of business. It was a trade with secrets and he was guarding his jealously. He said he would be delighted to show Freddy round but that he never

146

let anyone see his whole process. I got the feeling that Freddy would go madly for all the red leather-polishing and gilt-tooling but would die of boredom glueing thin string—and there appeared to be much more glue than gilt.

At the same time we thought about picture-framing and were lucky to know a friend who had a thriving framing business and we decided to make an approach to him if Freddy showed any interest in the idea.

We broached these subjects; Freddy discarded picture-framing out of hand and only showed mild interest in the book-binding idea.

'Incredibly noisy, oil to the armpits, formidable competition and the worst unions of the lot,' had been the opinion of two artist friends about the printing trade. Did I know the union still banned women? Freddy and I decided to find out for ourselves (about the printing presses not the women!). I had discovered two young men making a success of a private printing press and we set off to pay them a visit.

The young men put themselves out to show us everything. Work was being carried out in beautiful surroundings using old stables to house the presses and some high-class orders were being completed, some involving marbled paper and interesting print. Freddy wandered about looking at everything and the two young men treated him as their equal and were very pleasant.

I could see that he was not specially enraptured and it was fairly obvious that one would have to be extremely interested if not dedicated, as my artists were quite right, the noise was frightful and the oil was all there. It was also plain to see that intense concentration was required and I had doubts about Freddy's capacity for long-term concentration. Some time back our neighbour the cabinet-maker had helped Freddy with some very basic carpentry he was attacking and we had wondered then if he would show any leanings towards this craft. Our neighbour's verdict, when questioned about potential in this field, was that he did not consider that Freddy had the necessary staying power. We thought about this for some time and came to the conclusion that as well as interest in the work and a desire and determination to take pains and attain perfection, quite a high degree of intellect is required for sustained concentration and Freddy did not appear to be developing this kind of patience. He still assembled Airfix models meticulously but this was a question of following the instructions carefully and nowhere did any creativity come into the operation. If Freddy was having a day hacking at wood and it did not go right straight away, then he made do with his sub-standard effort.

We were both touched and amused by people who in their concern for Freddy also had an eye to their own interests. A very keen shot had just had his gun repaired by an old hand who bemoaned the fact that no young men were entering the trade these days and he could not see how it was going to end; and a violinist had the same sad tale—apparently no one was making violins any more. They were each convinced that they had found exactly the right job for Freddy to learn and though we never saw fiddles being made I did take him to the Game Fair where we stood for a long time at a trade stand watching gunsmiths at work.

It was interesting thinking up jobs for him, at times it even seemed like fun, but in fact none of the ideas was coming to anything and when I stopped and tried to imagine the detailed actuality of Freddy holding his own in a recognized trade, my mind just blanked out.

I experienced a timeless moment of querulous misgiving which merged from its timelessness into long time, which in its turn manifested itself in a sickening sensation that began in my feet and rose slowly but steadily through the whole of my body and settled itself thickly in my throat like glue. I gasped, I could not breathe, my head spun and I felt near to panic. It passed—I was clutching the top of some bookshelves ——the pictures settled themselves on the walls, the saints and knights from the brass rubbings looked solemnly and accusingly down. I remembered the old priest in Cornwall and I thought of Freddy as the person he was, with his gaiety, his spontaneity, his incredible patience and his marvellous enquiring mind. I felt bitterly ashamed of my uncontrollable fear and could not summon up enough courage to think of the women I knew and all those I did not know who also had Freddys or Fredricas, some with no husband to support them and a lot less of other things besides.

148

It was becoming dusky. The clock on the landing struck eight and ticked on, the shadows of my young in the empty rooms melted away and I was left alone in contemplation. I knew that what I wanted for everyone was that they should find out what they could do and then do it. Everyone can do something. How to find out about Freddy? How to help him discover his ability within a feasible context?

The room became quite dark and the air oppressive and then came a strange sound, unheard for over a month, of heavy single taps gathering momentum into a concerto of strong rain. My family were out, sleeping under the stars and this time they did not even have our tents!

I collected them next day from a point some twenty miles off. Freddy was gay with the achievement of the march and full of all they had seen in the way of birds and views. The night had been spent in a barn and they had stood under a leaking gutter next morning and enjoyed a natural shower. Freddy spent the rest of the week riding a hired horse in the forest and it was after this that we had made our Lundy plans and gone there to do the cooking job.

16

Heather returned from Madrid, sun-kissed and golden and almost unable to speak English. After unpacking she announced she must lock herself away for four days and write a thesis. I took her cue and removed Petr and Freddy. We went to Grandpa's farm. We had promised my father that Freddy would help with some ditch-digging and the time spent there in serious work was going to tell finally one way or the other whether he had the makings of a farmer.

We had never felt he had, and to us it seemed a bleak and solitary life. Freddy could not have coped with lectures at an agricultural college nor with all the book work and accounts that are part of modern farming. Apart from that, though he loved country life, he showed no real feeling for or under-standing of land as such. He was to be on the farm till the ditch got dug and, with an eye to a possible future on Lundy, I asked my father if someone could teach him to drive a tractor.

We had a happy weekend during which Petr tickled a small trout from the sizeable river along the boundary of the farm. He raced through the fields with it, as proof, wrapped in a handkerchief before sprinting back to return it—just breathing —to its natural home.

Freddy was impressed and amused by this episode, but also restive, as he just did not possess this kind of tenacity of purpose. Petr had stood in the icy water for three-quarters-of-an-hour while Freddy got bored on the bank: I wondered how the ditch-digging was going to go.

Petr and I left him starting on it on a Monday morning. The sun shimmered on the wet lawn in front of the old house. A thrilling haze promised a hot September day and we lowered the hood of the car. We were flashing down a motorway when Petr told me he had decided to stay in the West. The car was making 70 mph, but the world stopped. We did not want to get off, but life seemed to be turning into a series of startling events; I felt I should remember this time as the summer of extremes and I vaguely knew that it was a landmark for us all and that compared with this phase in our lives everything prior to it had been ordinary and I wasn't sure that anything would ever be ordinary again.

'I think you know that our home is yours for as long as you need or want it' I heard myself saying and, still slightly stunned, I did not catch Petr's reply until '. . . I feel like a brother to Freddy.' And this was good for them both, especially as he was going to be without his young Czech brother.

When Freddy came home with his gumboots lacerated and five pounds in his pocket, we all knew for certain that, along with game-keeping, farming was not for him.

He had completed the ditch and was proud that Grandpa had been pleased with him and the work, and he had put in about ten hours on a tractor. It was late September, the long hot summer was drawing to a close, the evenings were darker and autumn term was due to start.

'About your life,' I said to Freddy as we wandered through sodden ferns and grass under dripping pines in Lincolnshire woods one cold October Sunday. 'If they would have you, could you do a whole season on Lundy?'

'It's the best thing,' he replied. 'I'd like it for ever, but not winters. What would I do in the winter?'

'We thought you might enjoy work with horses. Somebody's hunting stables.'

'Yes, I think I would' he said, 'and I could ski when hunting finishes before I went to Lundy.'

'Well,' I said, 'if you really feel like that I'll write to Lundy and see what they say.'

'And you *must* tell me.'

'Yes, of course,' I assured him.

'Mum?'

'Yes?'

'You know, if I couldn't do Lundy every year I like forests and I'm thinking I could do forestry. I really like trees. But I'd like Lundy first.'

'It's a terrifically good idea and I'll ask Dad to find out about it,' I said.

Freddy had practically overcome his feelings of hopelessness; they had changed to determination born from alarm as he began to face his future for himself.

The people at the Priory and we ourselves all agreed that by the end of the autumn term Freddy would be ready to leave them. They did not feel they had anything more to offer and their school year began in January with an inevitable repeat of visits to places of interest, etc. Freddy had seen a year round there and we didn't feel he could benefit from further repetition. There was his last letter of the term and then home he came and just before he turned seventeen it was Christmas.

Dere Mum & Dad,

Thank you for the letters. I am well and in good form. I would like the base-board ready so that there is something to do if it is too wet a day. I would like to learn how to drive your car and more about the tractors with Mr W. I can't remeber how one had spelt it as.

The book Popski's Priavte Army I did enjoy very much. The bit of the two German tanks firing at each other I think was in African deserts, but a minor battle was fought in the mountain in Italy.

The house was full of people and I was not evern aloud to go besides leanding Mr L my gold cuffs from my Godfather. Why I was not aloud to go was that it was Latin. But I would enjoued it as well. Because they had some very good singners I was told. I was not very pleased about it.

The other day I saw a film called Alfred the Great. It was quit good but I would not want to see it again. To much of the story as I know it.

There has hardly been anything exsitting. But I made a sort of song poem . . .

Animal gives way to nothing,
People gives way to animals,
Horse and Master gives way to People
    and Animals,
Man and Bike gives way to Horse and
    Master and People and Animals,

Man and Car gives way to Man and Bike
and Horse and Master . . .
      People and Animals.

I think that it is rather stange and no sense at tall but if
you reread it again and say the sort of turne it might work.
The idea came from a dream that I had one night.
    I must stop now and do some more work. End of term is
coming soon.
                Best love from, Freddy.

Our Christmas began early because Heather was twenty-one
a week beforehand. The house was full of young people. They
occupied all our spare beds and most of the floor space as well.
Petr was home and also Luis from Madrid.
    When the twenty-first birthday party revellers departed, Luis
stayed on for another three weeks. He could speak no English.
Communication between us worked out in an interesting way.
He and Petr shared a room and their relationship developed
through playing chess together. My husband could follow
Spanish via Latin. As was the practice in his own country, so
with us he began and ended each day kissing all female members of the household and shaking hands with all males. I came
to rely on this; it also happened when leaving and returning
to the house, and I discovered that an incredible number of
variations in expression can be administered or received in a
formal kiss!
    As for Freddy, he and Luis developed an extraordinary hand-
shake involving elbows and twists, which became their special
ritual. I recognized something familiar here and was taken back
fourteen years to when he was three and had resolved his communication with the guest writers by the 'head game'. Thus Luis
and Freddy expressed their liking for each other and when they
met eight months later they saw each other, grinned and went
into a clinch.
    The girls—the only ones for whom no language was necessary,
both spoke Spanish!
    Over New Year friends came to stay and we read the old year
out with extracts from various books. The theme that time was
Winter. Our bookshop friends were with us and David and Ted's
family. Freddy was delighted to have the boys with him again

and the three of them spread about his room and integrated themselves into a quite impossible shambles before they had been in the house more than half an hour! They were all taking part in the readings and were suitably nervous with excited anticipation. They sat together, animated on the sofa.

Freddy had been flapping round for days working himself into a perfect tizzy about his reading. Did I think *this* was all right or did I think *that* would be better? My opinion was much too important to him and partly because of this and partly because I never seemed to get my head out of the cooking pots, I had brushed him off saying the readings had to be absolutely individual and that he had got to make up his own mind for himself.

When he was called upon to give us his choice, he opened *How Green Was My Valley* and read a lengthy chapter. It was a piece of high drama containing a deep social message. There were pulsating passions and extremes of physical and mental endurance. He did not read very well and forgot about punctuation, but to him it meant so much that he infected everyone there and we all held our breath and lived along with him as he stumbled over the words he could not pronounce but got us triumphantly out of a snow drift just as we were about to breathe our last. This was how it was with all his reading as he turned seventeen.

He read C. S. Forester's *The Gun*. He soaked up all the drama and lived through every horror, he got the message, the symbol of the gun, although he only understood a third of the words. Aphasia still lurked. At the end of it all he was quite unable to tell us where it had taken place. He had shown us though that he was receptive to feelings and we encouraged him to read all he could, convinced as we shall always be that some is better than none. He had imagination and it needed feeding. We were very pleased about this but we felt that splendid though this response to books was, he must be disciplined to take trouble to tackle the words he did not know and not go skipping through at speed. We saw this as all too easily becoming a habit he might never break, even after better comprehension had developed, and this seemed to us something very important so we set about trying to draw the line between demanding a certain standard and some conscious effort and yet not repressing his enthusiasm and desires.

17

Once I knew that Freddy was truly serious about Lundy Island my husband and I had a great deliberation before I wrote to the new owners. The island had been sold and as Freddy was not mature enough to manage living there on his own, we had decided that I had better offer my services with his and the two of us should go there together. He would have had to shack-up with the boatman and Merchant Navy types who were used to rough language and rough beer. Freddy was not yet ready to cope with this.

Bearing in mind that Freddy might be going to Lundy, my husband booked a berth for him on a cruise in the Sail Training Association schooner the *Malcolm Miller,* the sister ship of the *Sir Winston Churchill.* So I wrote to Lundy reminding them that Freddy would be a year bigger than when they had last seen him, could drive a tractor, was going to sea, and, we felt, was up to a man's job. As for me, I expected they would probably use me in the hotel kitchens, though I should have infinitely preferred my home in the old lighthouse. But the divers only functioned in July and August and we meant business, a whole season, and therefore decided we were prepared to do any of the island jobs required.

We spent a long time composing the letter and it was not without some trepidation that the envelope was sealed and sent. It meant that Freddy and I would have to be prepared to trip off, abandoning our home and head of family, but my husband and I were both agreed that, if they needed us and were prepared to have us, it was our one chance of giving Freddy the opportunity of showing himself—and who knew what might develop from that?

Since my husband's temporary post had ended he had spent a year working for his county's Association for Boys' Clubs and he had also taught for a term in a comprehensive school in a modern industrial town. He was marking time and waiting as usefully as he knew how until Freddy was successfully launched in life and he was free to do what he most wanted which was to deal in books. If Lundy accepted Freddy and me, then he was going to spend this solitary season preparing and launching his enterprise.

While we planned our campaign my husband opened a file on forestry. He began correspondence about this as we had not heard from Lundy, and anyhow we could not possibly bank on it as Freddy's summer work for life.

The Priory people had recommended that we make an appointment for Freddy to go to the vocational guidance clinic and he also wrote to them. My husband spoke to some friends who knew a lot about vocational guidance and who said the National Institute of Industrial Psychology was better. Letters were sent off to this body and also to the education officer at the Forestry Commission, applying for appointments and information.

In the first case the reply we received was as follows: '. . . Senior Advisor . . . does not feel we would be justified in accepting your application. The main problem for Freddy will be one of placement, and we cannot help in this respect . . .'

The Forestry Commission replied: 'Entry to the Training Scheme has been suspended and I do not know when or where new colleges will be established. Someone with poor hearing may find forestry employment both difficult and dangerous.' We imagined Freddy not hearing someone shouting a warning . . .

My husband then wrote to the Conservator of Forests in South West England . . . 'There are not any apprenticeship or training schemes available in the Commission.' He then went off to see the head forester working in our local forest in the section managed by the Forestry Commission: he said he was taking on no apprentices and was just waiting to pension off the people he had. One evening, the telephone rang and a friend, a farmer and amateur jockey, called a bluff 'Hello, is that you?'

'Yes.'

'I've been thinking about Freddy. Thatching or Farriery. That's all, give it a thought,' and the line was dead. It was another of our friends with an eye to his own interests as well as ours and it was warming and pleasing in every way.

My husband wrote to the Agricultural, Horticultural and

156

Forestry Training Board at Beckenham in Kent. '. . . probably he would have difficulty . . . forestry industry is small and opportunities are limited . . . at the moment there are no vacancies in England or Wales.'

He then wrote to the Dartington Hall Forestry Training Centre. They wrote a considerate and considered reply referring to the possibility of a vacancy in their 1970–72 course. None of this seemed very promising but we felt we had not yet covered all possibilities and were full of determination, it being Freddy's own idea and unthinkable that it should not be feasible.

My husband took him to the Economic Forestry Group at Berkhamstead. A letter came saying 'Since speaking to you on the telephone I am afraid that a policy decision has been made that we should not continue the New Entrant Scheme . . .' Nothing daunted, the two of them set off, thinking 'You never know when you actually see people' etc. They were received kindly enough but the company's policy decision was firm.

They returned late the same day, crestfallen and disconsolate. No young people were being accepted for training anywhere within this extensive firm, but they had produced the address of one of their nurseries quite near our town.

This was visited the following day. Young trees were being planted out and other shrubs besides and, though the foreman was keen to take Freddy on as a trainee, trees were Freddy's aim, trees in forests, and there was no guarantee that after a couple of years' working in the nursery he would be taken on in the tree department. It was a bleak part of the world and the foreman who had lived in the tiny village there for twenty-five years said he still had not been accepted into it and there was no one he felt he could recommend for lodgings. Freddy quailed visibly at the idea of learning the extraordinary Latin names of plants and shrubs and it all looked solitary and doomed to loneliness. Nothing there felt right at all except the foreman who was a very gentle Austrian.

We wrote to the Regional Secretary of the Timber Growers' Organization at Gillingham in Dorest. They replied saying there were no vacancies but would let us know if any occurred and we never heard from them again.

We were wishing we had heard from Lundy and were very much wanting a definite proposition from the forestry world.

Freddy went off to see the youth employment officer. He was not encouraging about forestry but said he would enquire and asked Freddy what he thought of a farming training. Freddy explained he had done some but would rather be in a forest. With reference to the farming the officer explained that boys who went in for this generally lived with the family of the farmer with whom they were learning and what did Freddy think of that. He replied that he had lived with a family in Lincolnshire and did not mind but went on to say that he liked people best who dusted and washed up straight away and got it done! He also said he liked to know exactly what time the meals were. We were amazed. We had no inkling that an ordered routine meant so much to him and the officer too was surprised and amused.

Freddy celebrated his seventeenth birthday with a Sunday lunch and he chose to invite three young men, all in their late twenties, all school-masters. These were people he knew from his father's school whom he had met from time to time and who were all particularly kind to him. He had been invited to their rooms for various social occasions and he felt they were his friends. They were gay and entertaining and they took notice of Freddy. He was enjoying telling them he hoped to do forestry, and it was patently clear that he needed this identity with a specific and recognizable training. It was vital social security. Once the forestry had been talked about it was difficult for these kind men to keep Freddy involved in the general conversation. He would try to follow, but very quickly got lost, misheard, misjudged, and misunderstood. Again and gain he would quickly ask me 'Is that the same as in the film we saw?' with reference to a passing remark and again and again he would be miles off target and I would quickly reply that I would explain later and then, when later came, I would not for the life of me be able to remember what it was we had been talking about.

One dark and raining Tuesday I said to my husband 'Why not go to Dartington and see them in person at their Forestry Training Centre?' He said 'Good idea' and he and Freddy threw their toothbrushes into a bag, took some bread and cheese, got into the car and went.

It was a last and final shot. When they had gone I looked

outside and the sky was blue-black. Rain lashed against the window panes and the trees in the garden swished and swayed and birds were gripping the branches in alarm. It turned icy cold and the world looked as though it would never be light again. In my mind I followed our little car along the dark wet roads, that little car with the two people in it hoping against hope and steeling themselves against disappointment. In my own heart I already knew the game was up and, as the room grew even darker, so too did my spirits.

Next day at tea-time my men returned. Dartington Hall Forestry Training Centre had been a hopeless delight. Lovely country, a highly organized centre, but the lectures, mathematics and book work involved in the course were away out of Freddy's reach. Tool barns with gleaming saws and hatchets hanging in regimented rows, libraries of books on the subject, all most attractive. Cheerful, helpful people, very considerate and understanding, no vacancies and once again the small warning that deafness in this game presented a real hazard. It really seemed that Freddy's idea for himself was no good. There was no one left to approach. He was forlorn and looked wistful, disheartened and dejected. By this time we were thinking about our farming friend and his suggestion of farriery but did not want to mention it yet as I knew that Freddy in his present state of mind would latch onto any idea, purely for purposes of identity.

I asked him how badly he felt about forestry and expressed for the hundredth time our amazed unbelief that in all Britain they had stopped recruiting people. He sighed and shrugged his shoulders and said: 'Well, I saw their books in Devon and I couldn't do the maths *ever*, but I did want to work in a forest. What about Lundy, Mum?'

What, indeed. I wrote again to the organizers and at last received a reply, but they had wholly misunderstood our request. Yes, they wanted me for the season to do all the trippers' teas and Freddy could come too and help, and we could have the old school to live in. It was truly exasperating. Serving teas on the days the Campbells steamers came was no job for a man. Freddy still looked very young for his years and I hastened to reply saying that certainly I would tackle the teas but that they must realize that as I had said in my first letter, Freddy was now a year larger, had learnt to drive a tractor, was about to join the *Malcolm Miller* and was more than up to a man's job and could they in the light of all this offer anything better and, if so, would they please let us know; time was precious and passing. We heard nothing.

And while the search for entry to forestry was on, do-it-yourself teaching had begun. Each day Freddy spent three hours in his father's study. The programme consisted of a reading-out-loud session followed by close questioning on comprehension. Then there was simple arithmetic with the accent on money and change. There was a news session after this and any interesting books relevant to the day's news were looked for and perused. Strikes in steel works led to books containing pictures of the industrial revolution which led to coal mining and on to ship building and what was happening on the land at the time, etc. Freddy had to produce several essays each week and the theme was accuracy and comprehension. My husband's findings were that Freddy at seventeen showed a very limited grasp of what he read and unless rather desperate pressure was brought to bear, his spelling, phrasing and general sense in writing his essays was extremely poor.

The weather was wintry and a figure to match it was seen with head down, a stumping step and an air of 'muttering' as it headed for its room and a half-hour of labour with the pen. All theoretical arithmetic involving symbols and problems or any kind of basic intellectual approach was out. X equalling O was still totally meaningless. His understanding of change for money did improve and I sent him to the shops as often as possible and he had to write down all the expenditures and answer for the change and gradually it became realized for him.

After lunch I tackled amateur speech therapy. We were driven nearly to distraction by his not pronouncing *-ing* properly and a lot else besides. I knew he could do it. He had got into very bad speaking habits. Since he was eleven and left the special schools where it was all laid on, I had failed to make other professional people realize the social implications of this situation. We could never understand why any mention of his poor speaking was invariably brushed aside. The first afternoon we began, I sat opposite Freddy across a table and looking strongly into his eyes I said 'Here is a green tin.'

'Yes,' he said expectantly.

'Well,' said I, 'every time you say *-in* instead of *-ing* you put fourpence in the tin.'

His face fell and his expression changed to one of sickened disgust. 'It's perfectly fair,' I said. 'You know you can do it and we've told you over and over again that if you want to get on with people and not go around sounding like a child of ten, then you've just got to do something about it, and you don't. But maybe this will help.'

He couldn't argue. He looked thoughtful and stony and then asked in even tones 'And what do we do with the money?' I was just about to say it could go in the church collection but that really seemed a bit too much so I said instead 'Well, when Petr comes home from the university the two of you could go down to the Red Lion one evening, couldn't you?'

A quiver of satisfaction crossed his face and he began to brighten up. I could see that our bargaining was terminated and that Freddy was going to settle. I gave him a newspaper article to read and we stopped and corrected all the faulty pronunciation and re-read it over and over again until it was as good as he could get it. He became very exasperated at times and fell back on the excuse that that was how he heard it. I said that I was aware of this but that it was not how other people heard it and that he must make the effort to use all the letters he saw in the words. Word endings melted away and *dog* sounded like *doh*, *fort* like *for*, and *d* and *g* together, as in *pledge*, came out like *pledth*. As for his *six* which sounded like *sieth*, I suddenly had inspiration. 'Say sick, Freddy' I demanded, and we had a brief moment of real low-down 'prep school' humour, both of us making noises of actually being sick and turning it all into a revolting burlesque.

The red herring was dragged back from its drain and I said 'And now add an *S*'. He said *sick-s* for the first time, properly. It was a thrilling moment and I was wildly elated with my absurd little success. 'Super,' I cried. 'Come on, now *Max*. Say *Mack* and add, the *S*.' He did so and I poured out a torrent of words for him to follow—*sticks, sixpence, exaggerate, exam, fix* etc., etc. That was a good day, but there were other combinations of letters which I wondered if he would ever master.

'You must listen very carefully when people talk and try and copy,' I implored. The word *asked* would come out *aksed* and numerous other letters got themselves in the wrong order. I became fascinated with the whole business and I learnt to listen very carefully myself. I have met a number of West Indians who all pronounce *asked* as *aksed* and wonder what, if any, the connection can be.

One afternoon we tried to fix *R*. He could not and indeed cannot pronounce his *R*s. We set about finding out how anyone pronounces *R*s. We gargled and gurgled and spat until we were scarlet in the face. We tried to arrange our tongues in places which seemed most unnatural when one analysed the movement, but for all this desperate physical exercise, Freddy could not do *R*s. One afternoon I said 'Try some wine' and poured us each out a small glass. But it didn't work. I was purring away like a giant tom-cat and making Freddy look into my mouth to see where everything was. I placed my hand under his chin to try to guide the movement farther forward. We could not get it and we'd done enough. I suppose I should have given him champagne!

But his speaking did improve and slowly he learnt to take more trouble. I often thought of the people in Lincolnshire and how cruel and extreme, if not downright shocking, they would have thought my methods, and it was very gratifying when Easter came and Petr was home to find only 3s 8d in the green tin. Barely enough for a couple of shandies, and the visit to the Red Lion never took place.

Freddy was riding horses very well but he had never fallen off and this rather bothered me as one knows it has got to happen before one can really get going.

I explained my concern to a friend who ran some stables and I asked her if she could take him out herself on a well and truly corned-up horse and do some jumps and give him a bit of a challenge. She agreed to all this and one sunny afternoon the two of them set out. 'It's no good,' she said when she telephoned me later. 'I put him on a really nervous thoroughbred and we went extremely fast. I took one jump and knew for sure that it would fix Freddy and with my heart in my mouth I turned round to see how he was getting on only to see him come flying over, the horse bucking and him hanging on like a monkey!' However, she telephoned again a few days later to say she had heard of someone nearby with a proper school who took people for courses and taught show-jumping and eventing.

We contacted this woman and in mid-February decided to have some intensive training. Still he did not fall off, but he learnt to get his seat down in the saddle and was kept hard at practice over a cavaletta and other obstacles in the school.

Mrs M was a born instructor, patient and explicit. Mid-February was not the ideal time for such activity and one day when I went over to see how things were going, there was Freddy on an enormous horse with whistling winds catching at strands of his hair, blue with cold and concentrating hard on the job in hand. I was told that after a poor start he had made enormous strides which had revealed a potential horseman in him.

It was the middle of March and one Friday evening we closed all exercise books for ever.

My husband's conclusions at 'the end of this do-it-yourself period were that with individual tuition vastly more progress could have been made, very much sooner. (It was for this we had sent him to Sussex and Lincolnshire.) As it was, his particularly limited potential had not been realized to its full, but at the same time any further attempt at formal learning would only have led to greater frustrations. Physically, Freddy was developing normally—there were arguments about his shaving more often—but he was most vulnerably aware of his limitations in every way. We had got him thus far over the last four years by our own efforts and expense, yet more could have been achieved if only those who had tried to teach him had really made themselves aware of the gaps in his basic knowledge, which they could have if they had only *listened* to what we told them. Everyone thought they knew better, and our frustration had been educationists with CLOSED MINDS AND FIXED IDEAS.

18

We made out a list of things to pack for the sea.

At the beginning of that week we had casually mentioned the idea of being a blacksmith. 'Don't say yes or no now,' we said, 'but think about it. It's fun, you put your fire and tools in a van and dash about shoeing in people's stables. And it's rare today actually to make any whole object and that's good.'

Freddy looked thoughtful and asked how long it took to learn. We said we weren't sure but would find out if he thought he was interested.

Three days later he looked at me and said : 'You know, Mum, I really do like the idea of a farrier. I mean, I get on with horses and I think it *might* be fun.'

I said that I thought that it was absolutely fine if it really appealed to him and that anyway he could think about it while he was at sea and if the others on board asked him what he did he could say he was thinking about being a shoesmith and see how it felt when he actually said it.

All week we were tying knots. The instructions said that the ship would not sail if any crew failed the knot test or failed to name all masts, sails and parts of the ship. At last it was Sunday and Freddy was ready in his best clothes, with his kit bag packed with Navy sweaters and gymshoes. We drove to London on a cold, sunny day.

We went to a Lyons Corner House for lunch, Freddy's last meal ashore for two weeks. He was very keen and filled with a thrilling sense of adventure. He emanated excitement and there was a light in his eye I had not seen since our dream time on Lundy Island. The last six and a half months had been a dark period, but Freddy seemed that day to be emerging from a tunnel to brighter light and it was good to see him so.

We were fascinated to see who ate Sunday lunch in a restaurant in London. A lot of families were meeting each other, tiny children and elderly grandparents, several lonely ladies and some strange solitary men. It all felt vaguely Continental. At one and the same moment Freddy and I spied a man with a hearing aid, the same model as his own. We were always pleased when other people wore them as it made him feel he was one of many. Freddy wondered if the man had had to pay the full price or had had a reduction, like himself. Another man came in with one, but his was the old model with the pink plastic string and Freddy smiled a rather patronizing 'bad-luck-old-chap' smile. A third man arrived with his aid, then an old lady and then four more men. This made nine people in the restaurant with hearing aids. By then Freddy and I were weak with suppressed laughter. My husband, too, was amused and definitely took part in the fun, but not as uncontrollably as us. It must have been trying for him sitting there with two feebly giggling people, but he is a very patient man and he put up with us most lovingly. Freddy then started to do a simply colossal sum and we finally decided there was about £675 worth of hearing aid in the room. 'Not counting the batteries,' said Freddy, 'or all the repairs!' Hearing aid batteries had recently gone up in price and this was a very sore point with him.

We reached India Dock and there were the two ships, the *Sir Winston Churchill* and the *Malcolm Miller*. They looked beautiful and tiny and the thought of them bobbing about the ocean, full-sail, in a March storm was absolutely terrifying. The crew numbered fifty, divided into three watches, and we shall never understand how so many people lived, slept, worked and ate in so small a space; but they did and only a few of them, Freddy included, slept slung in hammocks out of the way. Young men, all, it seemed, every inch of six foot tall, kept arriving on the quay. The instructors were everywhere, up the ladders involved in the rigging, dashing about with paint and Brasso. One stood on deck receiving the boys and crossing off names. We told Freddy he'd better jump aboard and report. He agreed. He suddenly looked very very small and his earlier excitement had turned to pretty sickening apprehension. But the reputation of these ships and the whole conception of the idea and ideals was so good that it was with full unflinching confidence that we wished him luck and heaved his kit bag over the railings after him.

We watched him join some waiting boys and give his name and then he disappeared below deck. Ten minutes later he returned. Gone was the smart suit and he stood on the deck in jeans and a navy sweater with *Malcolm Miller* embroidered in large letters across the chest and a green arm band denoting the watch to which he had been allotted. We longed to see the sails unfurled and this elegant craft slink away down the river, but this romantic happening did not apparently occur for some hours so, with a sense of deep satisfaction and in the sure knowledge that Freddy was in for a truly valuable and memorable experience and in good safe hands, we waved to a small sailor-figure who was not looking and made our way homewards.

The house was strangely empty without him and we found that we were *very* tired. Perhaps not so much tired as weary. There is a special kind of strain which goes with questing and with Freddy it was trying to find out why? and why not? and over all hung the unnerving question dominating our entire lives, *how* it was going to be for him. We could not admit feeling weary for long because there was a great deal to do. The first thing was another approach to the youth employment officer to see what he knew about farriery. As always, he was willing to help but knew nothing and suggested we write to the Rural Industries organizer. But he gave us the wrong name and address, he was months out of date and it was the secretary of our county's 'Industries Committee of the Council for Small Industries in Rural Areas' to whom we had to write, and discovering all this cost hours of time and took up several days.

They lent us a list, published by the Worshipful Company of Farriers. We then wrote to the company and bought a list of our own. This list consisted of all master farriers practising in England and Wales, and in order to have something to tell Freddy on his return, my husband paid visits to three men working within ten miles of our home.

We then had a long talk about Lundy. More than anything in the world I wanted that season there for Freddy. If his nose was going to be put to the anvil in the autumn, then I wanted him to have that glorious freedom, and everything else the island is, for the summer. They just did not and did not answer my letter and I found it increasingly difficult to be tolerant and understanding about their administration problems although I knew them to be manifold. It felt a long time since October when I had offered our services, and the very next month the season was to start.

We could not wait for ever because we had thought of an alternative to Lundy and that was to send Freddy to the Riding School at Porlock for a three-month course in stable-management and horsemanship. If he was going to take to the farriery idea then this should have stood him in very good stead in the same way that the *Malcolm Miller* sea trip was a preparation for work on Lundy.

We wrote to Porlock and received an answer by return. There had been one vacancy left and that had been offered to an American. If, however, we definitely wanted it, we could have it, but we must let them know within the next four days. What to do? My husband was very keen on Porlock and indeed so was I, but my bones were most reluctant to sign and seal so quickly. My husband said, quite rightly, it was too good to miss. He had lost all patience with Lundy himself and wanted everything fixed. I willed and willed my island people to communicate, but the post contained no puffin stamp next day and we wrote to Porlock and accepted the offer of the vacancy.

Two days later a letter came from Lundy saying they quite realized what a stupid mistake they had made about Freddy and that of course he was up to more than teas. They were offering him a man's job on the island for the season and were still glad to have *me* on the teas.

We were lucky to have got that last place at Porlock and we could not go back on our word. I wrote to Lundy with a heart lead-like with disappointment and a mind most frustrated with boredom about the whole silly business, saying it was too late. It was something which could have happened and which I now knew never would.

Once Lundy was definitely off, we could make plans for the rest of Freddy's summer. Whatever work he was going to do, we saw it starting about the middle of September and so we thought of things we hoped he would find interesting and pleasurable, things he might not get the chance to do again.

The first thing after the sea trip was some skiing, and Petr would come too.

We were receiving post cards from Freddy. They came from Amsterdam, Weymouth and Le Havre. They spoke of storms and having fun and hard work, in large scrawly writing.

Two weeks passed and it was time to collect Freddy from Portsmouth. He brought a tin of Dutch cigars from Amsterdam for his father and some chateau-bottled claret from France for me. He had had a surprising time. Surprising in that they had been so busy sailing the ship there had been no time at all to play cards and make friends. It had been all eat, sleep and sail. The crew seemed to have been mainly soldier and police cadets; no school boys because it was term-time. Freddy showed both contempt and disgust for two lads who had had enough by the time they reached Weymouth and walked off. 'They were wet,' he said, 'and they left their watch short-handed and that wasn't funny.' His hands and knuckles were all cut about from the nylon ropes and he had failed to find any enthusiasts wanting to go ashore at Le Havre so had gone on his own and wandered round the docks, bought my wine, had himself some Coca Cola in a café there and had not got lost. There was a vague story about some girl who seemed to have been sitting in a shop window in Amsterdam with nothing on, and for the rest he had enjoyed taking some photographs which were imaginative and good, and he had thoroughly enjoyed the whole business of the sailing. We felt the other boys had been a disappointment, we wished it had been a school trip, but it didn't *really* matter. We were back on Freddy's problem, the social one, and contemporaries might have made him feel inadequate whereas this crew were mostly older than he and he had certainly kept his end up.

Ten days later we received a report. 'Determination and self-confidence improved enormously during the cruise.'

When after three days we had just about talked the sea out, Freddy said he had been thinking and decided he would like to be a blacksmith. So we told him what we had done while he had been away and that he could go and see some of the men with his father before we went skiing. He was very pleased that Petr was to ski with us and he was pleased about Porlock and fed up about Lundy. 'Oh Mum,' he said, 'two days too late, *honestly,* and we wrote all that time before Christmas.'

'I know, I know,' I said. 'Let's just forget it and hope the *divers* want us to cook for them again. Porlock ought to be terrific and they'll get you falling off there all right.'

'Oh,' he said, 'do you think so?'

To which I replied firmly 'Yes!'

19

Le Havre looked bleak and grey in the early morning but Freddy
was alert and full of a sense of ownership, pointing out exactly
where the *Malcolm Miller* had lain at berth. We reached
Chartres in time for some coffee and with the wonderful smell
of French cigarettes in the air and the encouraging sight of
roadsweepers taking their eleven o'clock brandies and arguing
at the high counters in the cafés, we relaxed into that smiling
'first day of the holidays' feeling. We went across the square
to the Cathedral and Freddy said he remembered being there
before from camping journeys, and it was exciting showing Petr
his first French cathedral.

High up I spied a tiny detail in one of the windows—it was a
little man with fat arms baking bread. Next to him was a cobbler
and then a thatcher. I knew that the next must be a farrier and
sure enough there he was with his anvil and his horse. He seemed
to put a seal on things, that blacksmith at Chartres Cathedral,
and it was with a rare thrill of confidence in the future, my very
first, that I stepped from the darkness into spring light and across
the cobbles to the gift shops where I found my detail of the
blacksmith on very good post cards. I sent one of them there
and then to our farmer friend who had given us the idea. I have
always loved good omens and felt this was one and my best
to date. Freddy did not share my exultation. There was too
much that was unknown for him for such an extravagant display
of feeling.

The boys shared a room and we were back with the happy
camaradie which they had enjoyed together on Lundy Island.
They discovered a shop in the village selling enormous bottles
of coke infinitely cheaper than that sold in the hotel bar. They
made a fridge for themselves in the snow on the roof outside
their window and one evening when I went into their room to
collect the socks to wash, the whole window was filled by Petr

coming in from a visit to their freezer. He had a bottle of vodka out there too and there were a couple of evenings when peels of laughter were heard through their door and some cards and jokes were going on.

Freddy was still in a state of insecurity about his life and prone to resent criticism either of his ski efforts, his manners or anything else. He was going through a slightly mean phase and was extremely unwilling to part with any pocket money. This to me seemed wholly understandable in the circumstances. He felt he had so little of everything that he was jolly well hanging on to anything he *had* got. But it would not do, and we recruited Petr to talk to Freddy, man to man, about life in general and sharing in particular. This he did, in a very kind, firm, good way and, we felt, to some effect. He drilled Freddy on the form in pubs and how if you joined a group then you had to stand your round, etc. Freddy argued that by the time it came to him, he might not want any more to which Petr replied that you stand your round whatever or you don't go into the pub or you go in but drink your beer alone. Freddy didn't like it but he accepted it. They talked of other things too.

Freddy had been instructed in the facts of life along with the other boys at the Sussex School and I had had various conversations with him as I had had with the girls whenever questions relating to sex had arisen. He was keenly interested, in his own special practical way and totally objective in his attitude. We had hoped he might feel he could talk to Petr about these mysteries if his adolescence was creating any problems, but it didn't seem to be necessary. They shared the simple and obvious jokes and references. Freddy at seventeen, though fully developed physically, was *aware* emotionally but as yet immature.

All too soon the holiday was over and when we reached Le Havre it was dark and we would have become hopelessly lost among the cobbles and railway tracks if Freddy hadn't taken over calling 'Left here, now right and left again.' It was his acute visual observation back in action and he led us straight to our waiting ferry.

There was no time to lose on our return. Freddy had to be organized for Porlock. We had to buy a really good hacking jacket and some boots. A sunny, blustery Sunday dawned and my husband set off to Somerset with Freddy, booted and spurred and keyed up with anticipation. Freddy dug in at Porlock to a strict routine of early rise and stable muck-out, then instruction in dressage, riding and jumping, cleaning tack, lectures in basic veterinary surgery and horse anatomy, and a final stable cleaning with a repeat of work at 8.30 pm if it was not passed by the 6 pm inspection. Meanwhile my husband was following up, with visits, the names of the master farriers on the list sent by the Worshipful Company.

He naturally began with those near to hand. The first had a very good reputation but his son had followed him into the trade and they did not feel they had enough time spare to 'show a lad'. They were conscientious people and said that though they could use him he would need to be taught and it took time. The second shook his head saying very firmly 'Too busy', but he did promise to see a friend in the heart of the racing-stable country and ask him. Two weeks passed and then a telephone message came from this man saying he had been too late and his chum had just taken a lad on.

My husband extended his search to four neighbouring counties and proceeded to visit twenty-six men therein, but from those who weren't ninety-two, hadn't moved away or weren't already dead, he got the same answer that he had had from the locals. This became alarming. We were told on all sides that it was a dying trade, that farriers were worth their weight in gold, etc. and yet it began to seem as though we were never going to get in on it.

Nearly all the men my husband saw were of very fine calibre. Some were extremely tough and interested only in buying ready-made shoes, doing it cold at top speed and making a lot of money. But most of them were traditional and had been brought up by their fathers and were shoeing hot and seemed very happy in their work.

This was what was so attractive and what we wanted so badly for Freddy. Most men seemed to make shoes in the mornings and then beetle out with a small forge in a van and visit their various clients during the rest of the day.

We had a friend in Berkshire who was a trainer. He had seventy-four race horses under training and some magnificent stables. We were loath to ask him for help in our quest as we did not want to burden him with the embarrassment of having

to say 'no' if he did not think Freddy a fit subject to learn with
him. We knew he would have difficulty in appreciating Freddy's
situation and in my heart I knew that his not very good speech,
which so many people said I exaggerated in import, would be
treated as a deciding factor there.

However, as things were getting rather desperate and time
was passing all too fast, we did telephone our friends and they
heard us out and were very kind and interested. It was finally
decided that Freddy should be taken over for an interview
during the Porlock half-term. As we arrived, a string of horses
was coming in from the morning's ride and our friend with
them. It was a stirring and magnificent sight. All that beautiful
horse-flesh and those thousands of pounds' worth of delicate
legs! Freddy and his father disappeared to see round the
establishment and pay a visit to the forge.

While this was happening, our friend's wife took me round
another way. It was obviously a very happy yard. All was bustle
and organized busy-ness. I felt Freddy would thrive and respond
in this well-ordered discipline. There was a terrific atmosphere
of important purpose and urgent exciting responsibility. My
husband told me later that our friend had asked Freddy if he
could hear the change in the sound when he hammered iron.
He had had to repeat slowly what he had said and Freddy had
replied that he could hear a difference when he hammered
wood. Our friend then said that was good because the whole
clue to good shoeing lay in this vital factor. As the sound
changes when you hammer in the nail, so you know where you
have got to within the delicate interior of the foot.

The forge and the resident farrier had both been impressive.
Someone had come in to report that a certain horse would be
needing shoes that afternoon and the farrier had nodded
acknowledgement; he knew each animal so well that on the
instant he was able to knock up shoes individually to fit that
particular beast. We went to lunch. Our friend had at one
time in his career been an instructor at Porlock so he sat Freddy
beside him at the table and proceeded to ask him questions.
How many instructors were there and what were their names?
Freddy could answer the first question but he only knew his
teachers by their nick-names. There were other questions
referring to jumps, fields and routine, requiring specific tech-

nical answers which Freddy was unable to supply adequately and we could see that with so much at stake in a place like this, no-one could possibly run the risk of any mistakes being made and although *we* knew that given time Freddy, once he knew the form, would prove most responsible, we could see that if you did not know him as we did, this was hard to believe on the showing he made. He suddenly seemed terribly young, and trying to imagine ourselves being the trainer and not knowing Freddy, we had to admit *we* would have felt disinclined to take him. And so it was.

They were kind and showed real concern but they were in big business. Freddy returned to Porlock and set about the last phase of the course. These are some of the letters we received from him there:

> . . . all is well here so far. A test tomorrow which I hope will go well.

And

> Took a path home by the woods. Plesant but rather mudy. dots of primroses which brings that terriable name of the girl. I saw a most enormous flower tree full of the most beautiful flowers which we have by the tap and painting of in your room. A lot of Americans here. Mostly girls. Only three boys in one room which include me. Big John is quit nice very quite sometimes and is Irash from Irlande the other little John comes from near Manchester. Good, not bad but smokes at the table?!! Not nice, anyway no trouble from them yet. I am alright so far. Thank you for the holiday and did you and Petr enjoyned the Check play in London?

And

> Well, I had a fall for the first time, cellbrated myself at the pub down the road. . . . Had a beautiful weekend off. Bought J. her birthday present, a drying-up toole embroded with ABC etc to Z. Many hands make things easier with a very good autum Spring coulars which was the nices out of the few dull not makeking coalors.

I hope J will like it, O yes, what is HER address. It is aflul, allways lossing it and for getting it too. Disgraseful. Nothing can be done about it. Lazed around in the sun. Read the book Raven Seek Thy Brother. Good, rather depressing at times. Now I am reading the Jungle is Neutral. Very exciting until he loses his English helper the story went rather dull. It might clear up later in the book. . . . I went for a long walk to the costal station. It reminded of Lundy in which I could not see. Returned walked straight up the something beacon point. Fantastic view. Ran straight down until I saw a stream. A road bridge which turned out to be a foot bridge. As it was so hot I took off my socks and shoes, waded across. Beatiful feeling. It felt like something that one can only say for themselves because of the feel. Whashed my face in the stream and drank the running water. Walked all the way home by road not wanting ask a lift . . .

And

Money I am not too sure but I feel I ought to earn a bit more during the holidays talk about it at the weekend. I do my own washing up of clothes and the worse thing I have done is the towle. My, whate hard work!!! But to iron the thing was easy. The two Johns have not changed much but there is a very nice American girl who I like and had told me disadvantages and adventergions for girls in America. Must tell H these things before she goes. Can't write it out. To much to put down simply.

And

I took my films to the young barman as he wanted to see them as he had done a bit of sailing, but not quite so big as this.

Here Freddy referred to his *Malcolm Miller* photographs.

Then a very nice man came for a short time, saw them and asked if he could look at them. I said yes and expleind it all. He was interested and then said afterwards. I like people who take the trouble to say what they know of what they had exsperonced and take a kneen interest of what they had done. He would loved to know more but had to leave. I think I have seen some swallows. Can't quit make out which it was. I have already started to press flowers (wild) Could you tell me how you should do it please. Are the birds in the nest yet. The one below Petr's window.

At the end of it all an examiner came down from the BHS and examinations were taken for the Assistant Instructor's Certificate. The colonel in charge of the running of this course was so pleased with Freddy that he said he was going to explain to the BHS that he had speaking and writing difficulties and ask for allowances to be made in his case because of the good show he had put up on the job during the three months.

Apparently all the instructors were in agreement with this plan as they had found Freddy painstakingly keen and careful, and enormously improved in the saddle since his arrival. So the great day came and the examining began. Freddy reached the pass mark and came home the proud owner of an AI certificate which we promptly had framed.

In the meantime, my husband, after several more visits to farriers he heard of through other farriers, ran one to earth quite nearby who was in the process of moving even nearer and who agreed to take Freddy on. The arrangement was that he should go for a fortnight's trial, see how everyone got on, then break for a week as we had an arrangement to go on a canal which we could not alter, and then start in properly, provided the trial run had been a success. This man was planning to buy a pub and, working with his brother-in-law, put the forge at the back of the inn running the two projects together. He had been trained in the army with a cavalry unit and had a number of army polo ponies on his books as well as the odd racehorse and the usual run of hunters, stud farms and ponies. It all sounded promising and when Freddy came home my husband took him over to meet this master farrier and set about getting him driving lessons, as a small van was going to be vital for everyone's independence.

176

20

Heather had received her degree in Edinburgh and joined by Jean we had all gone up to Scotland to watch Grandpa fish. Various cousins were there including two boys from South Africa, one older, one younger than Freddy, and he was looking forward to meeting them and exploring the river. The encounter was disastrous. The boys made a bee-line for Freddy's sisters. Their parents were sweet to him all the time and talked to him about his life but it was the young with whom he wanted to count. We could see all too plainly how this situation happened. The South African boys were sophisticated and their interests were sport and cars. They lived so much in the open in Africa that exploring the banks of a Scottish river on a cool grey summer's day held no charm for them. With the girls they shared a zany student language, in-jokes and weak wit, but communication with Freddy was virtually non-existent and he was left to string along as best he could. He felt this badly and all the splendid confidence gained at Porlock began to dwindle away, and on the last day when we were sorting out in which car who should travel, Freddy came to me and said 'There's no point in me going with Jean and Henry, they'll be talking together *all* the way and I don't like it.'

There was nothing I could do or say. We had stood by helpless, witnessing his humiliation, and wishing ourselves a thousand miles away and knowing it would be exactly the same there! No blame to Henry and Charles. They were oblivious. They did not know Freddy and probably thought him a quiet retiring type and were leaving him alone. 'Would it be too sickeningly dreary if you came with us?' I asked. 'It's a lovely day, we can put the hood down and we'll arrange to meet the others outside Perth for lunch. It's easy to get on with people at picnics.' Freddy thought a while. He desperately wanted to be with and of 'the young'. 'I'll come with you' he said flatly.

And then it was time to equip him with working clothes. We had made endless enquiries in the village he was going to, to find him digs, but there did not seem anyone willing or able to take in a lad for four nights a week. Not that and feed him as well. He was nowhere near taking his driving test at this stage, so the first morning he and I set off at 7.40 after our breakfast and he tied his bicycle onto the back of the car as we had decided he could cycle the five miles back. It was a beautiful morning and I left him at the forge keen with anticipation.

He cycled into the yard that evening looking pleased. The day had gone quite well—but he had reservations. 'The language,' he said, 'is incredible, every other word begins with F and I don't mean fantastic.' I had to laugh. There stood Freddy, the shoe-smith's apprentice, propping up his bike in the late summer sun, wearing his new TUF shoes, old jeans and darned jersey and his face smeared with grime from the forge, at the end of his first day's work and the beginning of his adult life.

We were sorry about the swearing and felt it must be pretty bad for him to mention it so forcefully. He knew that some men swear and had met it farming, boating and in moments of various people's stress. If the man was going to swear so continually we could have wished him to be a 'B' rather than an 'F' man but perhaps that was simply a question of non-taste. Next day we did it all again and this time when Freddy returned he said he had been allowed to remove some shoes from a horse but that the man had stood over him telling him to hurry as 'time was money'. A tiny ominous dart struck my breast.

Freddy also told us that he had to be on the job by 6.30 the next morning. 'Right,' I said 'early bed and up at 5.15.' After leaving him at the forge I stopped in a field and gathered mushrooms on my way home. 'Morning picked' I said to myself: 'More like middle of the night!'

When Freddy returned early that afternoon there was no light in his eyes and his step was heavy. 'What is it, darling?' I asked.

'Oh, he swears all the time' he said.

'Well, why do you mind so much?' I asked with a sinking

heart and I knew he was really protesting about something quite different.

'Well,' he began and then went on, 'he's always in a mad rush and shouts about getting a move on and can't I get them off quicker than that? And, well, he's never shown me how and I don't know how to do it because I've not done it before and then he's angry and the swearing gets worse and I've got to be there at 5.30 tomorrow.'

'5.30!' I exclaimed. 'Why so early again?'

'Because of the polo ponies with the Army. I will be finished at 1.30 pm, but I don't want to be finished then. I think it's because he wants to paint his pub.'

I agreed with Freddy that these hours were not good enough, particularly as my husband and I were going to the theatre that evening and could not hope to be back before midnight and I was losing out on sleep. 'However,' I concluded, 'for this fortnight, let's not say anything but just do exactly as you are told and then when he and Dad have their talk about the future we'll jolly well get it put right and say we want reasonable working hours.' Sure enough, I flopped into bed at twelve and crawled out at four. There was a mild drizzle making the morning grey, which turned into a steady stream as we reached the forge on the dot of 5.30.

The place was deserted and there was not a light to be seen anywhere.

'Are you sure you got the time right?' I asked, because Freddy did, very often, get messages wrong.

'Yes' he said in a voice absolutely confident on this point.

We sat in the car outside the building watching the day getting slowly lighter and wetter and then at 5.45 I told him to run into the forge again and look around at the back of the house. Still nothing. I suddenly knew I was not going to leave him in that place alone waiting and I did not feel I was being soft. We left a note saying we had been and waited and gone. At 5.55 we left.

Freddy's eagerness to fall in with my plan was all too evident and his face showed that going home again was a simply splendid idea. Not for the first time the bottom was beginning to drop out of our world. As I hung on to the steering wheel, the familiar sensation of fear began. Creeping fingers of panic

179

were gripping my heart and it was through clenched teeth that I said to my husband as I woke him up 'He wasn't *there.*'

'Oh *no,*' replied my very patient man. 'That really is *too* bad. I'll have to go and see him.' It was 6.20 and at that moment the telephone rang. A gruff voice demanded where Freddy was. Did the voice not find the message left in the forge? We had been and found no one and had come back.

'A man can oversleep' came the reproachful retort. 'I wanted him down at M. We're doing the polo ponies.'

My husband said he wasn't prepared to argue at that hour and would the angry voice please telephone him at 6.30 that evening. Freddy was standing in our bedroom with an enormous question mark on his face. We could see how completely torn he was. In his heart he knew as well as we did how vital it was that he have a job in life and that there were not many that were interesting and that he could manage. At the same time he was hoping against hope for some miracle to happen that would mean he did not have to go back to that forge. Well, he got his miracle though at this stage it was a wholly black one. I said to my husband : 'You know, I think we have got to show willing for these two trial weeks, I think we ought to take Freddy down to M now. I'll go.'

'No' said he, 'I mean yes, I agree, but *I* will take him.'

I was so sleepy and felt so wretched that I kissed them both, kicked off my shoes, rolled under the bedclothes and prayed for oblivion. One hour later, at 7.30, I was woken up to find Freddy back home again. He had directed the way to the stables in the army camp where the angry voice and his brother-in-law were hard at work on the ponies. My husband had greeted them with a 'good morning' though it was apparent that the angry voice was pretending not to have seen them.

'Here's Freddy' my husband had said. 'He came at 5.30 as instructed but my wife brought him home again when no one was there, thinking he had probably made a mistake about the time you arranged. We are very much aware that he can and does make mistakes when he hasn't heard properly, but that is something we talked about when I first came to see you. Anyway here we are.'

The man had barely looked up and then replied, with his

eyes still on his work, that he 'wasn't interested.' So there had
been another journey home in the rain. This time Freddy was
really shaken. Now that the die was truly cast the way he had
wished it, security had gone with it and he was back to being
a 'no boy', suspended in life, experiencing the ghastly truth
that most victories are defeats, particularly the minor ones; and
when he saw and heard me let out a low despairing cry of 'Oh
no, Oh no', roll over onto my stomach and pour huge tears
into my pillow, he was really unnerved.

'Mum,' he called. 'You're crying, *don't*, why?' This with a
break of near laughter in his unbelief.

'Because he's so *horrible*' I sniffed. 'How *could* he, how
could he, how *could* he,' and I told everyone to go away and
leave me and that I would stop soon. I felt it would be never. I
was so tired, so desperately disappointed and so frightened, I
found I could not stop. Just when I thought I had got control
of myself it all began afresh.

For the very first time I completely gave way over the
Freddy situation and from the safe distance of this present
time, I can clearly recall a primitive response to what was
happening.

I was a Celtic keener, an Egyptian wailer and I was mourn-
ing the fate of all handicapped children and of their parents,
and of everybody who suffers from being discriminated against
by UNTHINKING SOCIETY.

I got out of bed and outside it was lashing with rain and
the flowers were being knocked about. I felt like the most
God awful hangover and crying was coming again when I
remembered the old man in Cornwall and the service when
Freddy was three. It was very difficult to believe in it all, that
disastrous and dismal morning, and I did not know that I did
believe. Then I knew I had to, and then I could no longer
tell what indeed was the meaning of belief. Was belief necessity?
If so I thought it seemed all right, so okay, I believed. And
then I got downstairs and it felt like about lunchtime, so much
had gone on, but it was really only breakfast time and the
thought of all that rain and a whole ghastly day stretching out
in front like the beginning of some impossible exam was too
much and I was looking helplessly round me wanting only that
life should *stop*, when Freddy burst in.

In his bewilderment and faced with this quite new situation he had not known how to react, but had felt a strong urge to do something, so he had shot out on his bike and cycled around till he had found a newsagent's open and had bought a small bag of sweets. He gave them to me and his expression as he did so clearly told me that these were to make me better and that they had better work because he didn't like it. And then Mrs Williams came in—she helped me with the house some mornings and she was a good *friend*. She most patiently listened and while I poured out the whole saga to her, I began to feel better. What with Freddy's sweets which by then we were all eating, and Mrs Williams's comforting remarks like 'Better now than later' and 'He couldn't be a nice man at all,' and 'What a way to treat people', some warmth was filtering back into life and I said to Freddy that as it was such a filthy day what about going to the cinema? This was a good idea so we set off after lunch.

My husband had long ago said goodbye to another 'working' day and was off into the countryside looking up the farriers we had liked best of those we had already seen, to make quite certain there was no change of scene and that they still could not take Freddy.

The cinema was meant to cheer us up but the film was *Kes*. I sat frozen in my seat as the story unfolded itself exposing the appalling results of a sensitive child at the mercy of a home background and a system of schooling which crippled him for life by the totality of non-understanding.

Freddy said the classroom and playground scenes reminded him of his time at our local school in the class for the backward and I crept from the cinema numb with cold and feeling terribly sick. The symbolism of the big bullying brother killing the bird didn't apply only to the boy in the film.

When we got home and my husband had returned with, not unexpectedly, no good news, those old clock people were back in our lives and up to their tricks again. After about three lengths of day, this one eventually crawled to a close.

'It's not the children who are handicapped,' I said to my husband as we lay in bed that night, 'it's the System and the Grown-ups.' We drifted fitfully into the uneasy sleep of the emotionally exhausted.

Unbelievably there *was* a silver lining to this cloud and it appeared five days later. A friend, farming and keeping eight horses in livery, had just lost his girl groom and was looking for another. He had a Porlock standard in his stables but it was difficult to find really good girls. We made an arrangement. Freddy was to work for him until either we found a farrier or he a groom and we hoped our missions would be completed simultaneously. Freddy looked pleased, but before all this happened there was our final item in his season of 'interesting fun' and that was the week on the canal.

After the disappointment of the season job on Lundy, we had hoped to go back and cook for the divers but they were having an economy campaign and two girl divers, wanting to attend the course but finding it too expensive, had volunteered to do the cooking in return for free diving.

In view of this, we felt the experience of Inland Waterways would be good and so, leaving my husband working on a book catalogue, we set off to the Midlands to board our craft. Freddy and I loaded our belongings and stowed them away in our little water caravan. We placed our provisions in the tiny well-equipped kitchen.

I left Freddy learning instructions from the manager on how to drive our craft, gauge petrol supplies and fill up with water and other vital necessities. We had had lock instructions sent with the confirmation of our booking, so had done our homework on them previously. I set off to Birmingham to collect Petr from a train and we joined Freddy and all set off at about seven in the evening.

I had primed Petr about Freddy's disastrous experience at the forge and he was very sorry and appalled at the potential consequences and the effect on Freddy's morale. When we had been chugging up the canal some time, Petr said to Freddy

'Bad luck you had with that chap, Freddy, what was he like?'

'Oh' said Freddy, 'swearing all the time.'

'Well' said Petr in his most provocative Czech way, 'you don't want to take any notice of that. Man's world you know.'

'Well, I know,' replied Freddy, 'but there were other things too.'

It was curious how he was so obsessed with the swearing business. We are not a swearing family but I did recall how much Petr had used 'blooty' in his talk on Lundy and the surprise which Freddy had registered when he noticed me letting it go. Petr's use of 'blooty' was just sloppy schoolboy talk and it sounded so funny said in his broken English.

Perhaps the farrier swearing had shaken Freddy's foundations a little and given a jolt to his security?

It was almost dark when we approached Kidderminster. Freddy had been put in charge of the boat in honour of his past experience and we had safely manoeuvred our first lock. There was the thrilling experience of being at a level quite separate from the rest of the world. We chugged under an iron road-bridge. It was low and the traffic hammered and clattered over us in an exciting, frightening way. When we emerged we were above houses and below the road. The lights from the town reflected in our water-path, swallowing, gulping and gurking in the night breeze, disturbing the surface. The rules said one was forbidden to travel by night but we had set off so late and could hardly moor in the middle of Kidderminster, so we drove on with stealth and a roguish sense of breaking the law. As soon as the last factory was well behind us and our one beam light showed up the trees and reeds and undergrowth of the canal bank, we found a mooring place and tied up.

We had imagined calling at canal-side pubs and having merry evenings but as it turned out we all seemed to want only to get into a quiet stretch of water, deep in the countryside, pull in, eat our supper and make our own jollity. This consisted of a desperate Czech card game which Petr taught us and to which we became wholly addicted. Freddy very often won and this was good for his morale. After the disastrous week with the farrier his confidence had plummeted again and that old apprehension and mistrust had returned. It made him irritable and Petr and I kept telling him gently, if we had the patience, but more often rather desperately, that everything he said came out in a cross voice. 'Well, I'm *not* cross' he would answer even more crossly, and we would say 'But you *sound* fantastically cross, so do try to change your voice.' It was a bad time for Freddy and I tried to cheer him by being encouraging about the grooming job he was going to. 'You don't seem a bit pleased about it' I said.

'Well,' he replied, 'I don't know what it's going to be like, do I?'

Everybody who has been afloat on a canal knows what fun it is to see all the fishermen sitting it seems for ever on the banks. There are the children who run endlessly up and down the towpaths, the little gardens and gnome homes seen from this unexpected angle and (out in the country) the chugging along above cow-grazing level and looking down on the countryside, the views seen framed in bridge arches and the cuttings in rocky places and the glory of sun shining through overhanging trees. All these things we soaked in, between our reading and card playing and boatman- and locksmanship.

At one moment there was a flower-name conversation. Petr was writing down the English names of flowers and from it we made the discovery that Freddy had always thought carnations were coronations. I wondered just how many more miswords he still had in his head.

The week was soon over and we were through Kidderminster again. It being light this time, we noticed more than on the outward journey. We steered our boat round corners where the canal twisted between the walls of grisly Dickensian factories. Blackened brick-face towered above us and prison-like windows looked down on us through bars. As we emerged into the homeward stretch to Stourport, mallow plants with their exploding seeds began to grow again at the feet of silver green willow trees. Suddenly Petr gave a shout. He had seen a rope hanging from a tree across the towpath on our left. We reversed the engine and went to investigate. Both boys climbed out onto the bank and ran through the willows to see. There was a fast flowing river which looked as though it was solid with thick chemical factory sludge. Someone had strung up the rope so that if you could get it over to your bank, you could then have a great time doing a Tarzan across the water. The

185

problem was how to get the rope. With the aid of the boat hook, Freddy's gum boots which reached higher up his legs than Petr's, much shouting, alarm-cries, laughter and shipping off of logs and branches dragged into the water, the precious rope was ours. Freddy was the first across. He did not hold the rope high enough up, and as he swung madly across with his knees under his chin, his hind quarters hit the sludge with a thwack and the filthy stuff splashed up and over him in a monstrous mud wave. The boys both became hysterical with laughter over this event, and then it was Petr's turn and though he had heeded the warning and had his hands placed high up the rope, he was so heavy the rope sagged and there was a repeat performance. Their laughter rang up and down the banks, peal after blessed peal. Once soaked, they both gave themselves up to it and swung across the sludgy river until they were tired.

I had retired to the boat to read, and when these two soggy and exhausted bodies presented themselves on the towpath I told them to strip and handed out a bucket of hot water and some soap. They proceeded to scrub themselves, still laughing, and then suddenly Petr's face clouded over. 'And what about our clothes,' he said, 'all those chemicals, do you think they will still be here in the morning?' I said I very much doubted it but that I would wash them with special care.

The following Monday Freddy was off by 7.40 armed with his lunch box for work at the stables. We took him there and, as with the farrier, Freddy had his bike on board for the return journey. Nearly always he did the driving as practice for his test.

He spent five weeks in the stables and very happy they were too. He had in David the perfect person to work for. He was kind and firm and friendly. He had superb standards. One could have eaten one's lunch off his stable floor and powdered one's nose in the reflection from his polished harness. The horses were superbly well cared for and Freddy was exercising twice a day in the forest as well as doing stable work.

During this time, we were, of course, still not finding farriers, but one day when my husband paid a visit to an elderly smith we had already seen twice, things began to look more hopeful. This man had taken a real interest in Freddy.

He could not take him on himself as his younger son was

186

already in his third year of apprenticeship and the two of them were managing adequately, but he thought he had heard a rumour that three young men he knew working together were looking for a lad. They weren't, but they passed us on yet again.

My husband set off to see this man. He was twenty-eight and lived and worked in a tiny village twenty-five miles away. He was not even on the list sent us by the Worshipful Company although he was a fully paid member and a qualified master. His brother had been working with him for three years but had not found it interesting enough to work an apprenticeship proper and was about to emigrate to Australia. This was the reason for John (as he came to be to us) needing someone. My husband came home saying he had liked everything about the place, and he had made an arrangement to take Freddy over for an interview. Freddy had Thursdays off from the stables, so on one of these the two of them went. My husband had introduced Freddy to John and had then left them together. A racehorse had apparently come in for plates, and Freddy had watched the completion of the job and then John had talked to him.

When they came home again I asked 'Well, and what was it like?'

'Oh, nice' said Freddy without any hesitation. 'He was doing a racehorse. No swearing.' He added with emphasis 'Except by the groom who brought the horse—and no mad rush and panic. I'm sure he won't keep saying "time is money" and then I can get on better because I know that time is money but you don't have to say so all the time.'

I asked him what the forge was like and he had been impressed by everything. 'He told me I'd have to find digs, Mum. He said he understood about digs because he had had to have them when he trained in Devon and he said I *could* live with them but that if I worked with him and we saw each other all day, he thought that would be enough and what did I think.'

'What *did* you say?' I asked, wildly curious to know the answer.

'Well,' he replied, 'I said I quite agree.' So there seemed to be a pretty good understanding already established between these two and it was arranged that Freddy should report for duty on 19 October.

There were a few weeks to go and after so many abortive

attempts to get the right thing off the ground, we did not dare relax into total belief that all was truly safely 'in the bag'. At the backs of our minds was the nasty lurking fear that still something could go wrong. I remember thinking that this was how it must feel for the first three months when people adopt a baby and the natural mother can still claim it back and so they dare not love too much and yet cannot help doing so. While we kept telling ourselves there was plenty of time for anything to happen, yet it all felt good.

And surely enough the 19th of October dawned. David and Freddy had a tremendous 'au revoir' mid-day-pint session in their pub. David had a girl coming the following week so all had worked out well there. Freddy came home saying for the umpteenth time what a grand person David was and how much he liked all his friends in the forest.

'Well you see, my dear, it's the bathing and that' she said darkly as I stood among her begonias in the early autumn sunshine. I had heard the village was not on main drains and was aware it must be these to which she referred. She was the seventh person on whom I had called as I was trying to find lodgings for Freddy. I hastened to explain that warm hearts and good cooking meant more to us than any flushing loo, but she remained vague and darkly referring.

If I thought questing was over I was mistaken. I saw everyone on the list given me by the postmistress and then I started on the town. Nobody wanted a worker—not even a four-nights-only-a-week one, and definitely not one smelling of hoof parings, iron filings and coke at the end of the day, and needing baths as well as an evening meal and a packed lunch. The landladies either had students from the *Royal* College who did not need cooking for, or Concorde *gentlemen* whose status made cooking worthwhile. Bosoms heaved with self-righteousness and doors were closed with smug self-satisfaction.

I left notices in supermarkets but they drew no response and I ate a number of lunches I did not want in pubs as they were the best places for the gossip. I can no longer remember how we came upon the lady who said she would take Freddy. She agreed to everything with alacrity but added that it could not be for long as her house was up for sale. He was happy there with this neat person, her neat house, neat cacti in rows in the tiny, neat porch and her friendly dog.

We took him, his bag and his bike and it was St Luke's day when Freddy began working with John. After a couple of weeks he brought an important-looking document home with him and this was his apprenticeship papers laid out in beautiful 'Tom Jones' language and we all read it and he duly signed on the dotted line, promising to do no damage either to his master or his property and pledging himself to move at least ten miles away if starting up on his own at the end of his time.

Things went well at the forge from the word go. John was kind and calm, patient, encouraging and generous. He had humour and he took endless trouble showing Freddy how things went, without any visible signs of irritability.

Time *is* money and although it was in John's interest to turn Freddy into a useful man, it is always quicker and easier to do it yourself as I knew full well from my total failure to teach the girls how to cook.

There seemed to be a tradition that if a horse won a race a little something from the prize money came the farrier's way. John would share this with Freddy and if there had been an extra hard week there was often extra in his Friday envelope. Freddy was tremendously proud of this and it gave him a most desirable sense of being a vital cog in John's works. He responded with an important development in his sense of responsibility and on Friday evenings when he returned home he straight away went to the kitchen, put out his lunch box, put his working clothes in the wash house and then cleaned and polished his TUF shoes ready for the following Monday morning.

Freddy has never once had to be called twice at 6 am on a Monday and we have never once left the house in a chaotic mad rush. This is something quite new and is the measure of respect he has for John and his job. The work is extremely hard and very dirty and he has never shown the least signs of boredom or a falling-off of interest.

Freddy is doing 'his thing' and a more perfect 'thing' with a nicer master would be very hard to find.

John has a wife who is as nice as he and she often spoils Freddy with cups of tea and thirds of whole homemade cakes. There is a dog, a happy three-year-old Michael and a baby.

The whole family spent a Sunday with us recently and someone who came in to meet them asked John how he had assessed
Freddy's ability for the trade. He replied that before the first
week was out, he knew that Freddy was a lad who would 'hang
onto a hoof'. He elaborated further by saying he could tell that
if he got kicked out of the window, he would be taking the
horse with him and, the best music of all in our ears, he said
he could already tell he was going to be good.

I took Freddy over one Monday, and as we arrived the light
was coming, and the trees in the village were emerging through
the winter morning murk. Freddy got the fires going with the
chips left by John for the purpose, and John came over and
their day was begun. I said my goodbyes and outside the forge
the light had changed to a delicate pink. There was an audible
silence hanging over the village and though barnyard fowls
have left the country scene, the birds were busy. I stood soaking
in the silence and feasting my eyes on the beauty of this place,
with smoke beginning to rise from cottage chimneys and a new
day stirring as lights went on in windows.

It seemed like a miracle that all this had come about, and
come about so well. John can never know what it means to us
to have found him. He has built-in compassion with total understanding. He is not conscious of these graces because they are
just part of him.

I heaved a huge sigh of simply colossal gratitude and excited
disbelieving belief and my heart sang till I thought it would
burst as I drove the miles home.

With the unique pride, confidence and independence that
comes from earning your money, Freddy was taking three ladies
out to dinner. They were the head of his first school, the speech
therapist and his other teacher.

The children had left for the holidays that day, we were
staying there and Freddy was sleeping in one of the little beds.

'Remember the tadpoles?' they asked. We were deep in shop
talk while Freddy spruced himself up for the evening.

'We had everything' they said, 'portholes, flag poles, frog
poles, but *never* tadpoles.' They also reminded us of Freddy
going 'bird washing' and learning to use binoculars. They had
studied the story of Pinnochio and Freddy had got hopelessly

confused trying to write a letter to us, thinking that Pinnochio and binoculars were one and the same thing.

These were the three people responsible for teaching Freddy how to speak. Still devoted, still dedicated, passionately interested and full of warm humour and enthusiasm. I had forgotten the tadpoles but we reminisced about the Cinderella pantomime.

'Please tell us tomorrow,' I said, 'exactly how you find him. So many people tell us he's absolutely all right, but we know differently. The other day I heard myself saying "We must strike while the iron is hot" and then realized that the phrase can only have originated in a forge, culled by simple, illiterate men hundreds of years ago. I could *not* get Freddy to understand it. To begin with there was confusion with the postal *strike* that was going on. But after we had sorted that out, he still could not reach the meaning of the phrase either literally or symbolically. How can this be when he gets the finer points of an intellectual film like *Women in Love?* He understood Lawrence's passion for nature and recognized Gerald as a most unhappy man who couldn't love.'

Next day we found a moment when Freddy was not in the room. 'It went fine!' they said. 'We guessed that his father had taught him the drill about ordering dinner and he bought a bottle of wine. His disability,' they continued, 'is camouflaged by social "know-how" but it's there, aphasia still lurks, and the answer to your question is that a film is visual and appeals to the emotions and is intuitive, whereas he cannot see patterns of words in his mind, nor therefore transfer their symbolic meaning.'

This is aphasia, and it is impossible to tell whether Freddy will ever develop well enough to run his own forge, with the complications of telephone messages, people's names, ordering materials, training lads, and keeping accounts.

But he is now driving a car. And he 'fired' for John in the shoeing competitions at a big show not long ago. As John was judged, so I feel should Freddy be—VERY HIGHLY COMMENDED.

Epilogue

We had been struggling with Freddy's life for sixteen years and this was the first time we had been able to look ahead in terms of some long time. An extraordinary calm settled upon us all. It was full of peace and security. The bugle had sounded 'cease fire' and I could afford to listen to the birds singing. We were overwhelmed by this luxury and as my husband sank deeply into his work, knowing he at last had long stretches of uninterrupted time ahead of him, I turned my thoughts to the three mothers who had responded to Gillian's article and whom I had seen with their children. What was happening? How were they getting on? I now had time and a mind clear enough to pay attention and I wrote to them all. From the mother who brought her five-year-old to see me, I received this (the little girl was now eight):

. . . How nice to hear from you after all this time. I often wondered how Freddy was progressing and am delighted to hear of the apprenticeship. I wish him every success for the future.

I am afraid our news is very sad. K was eventually diagnosed as suffering from a rare and fatal brain disease called mucopolysaccharidosis.

After the diagnosis and prognosis (she had about five–six years) was made I decided that I simply couldn't cope with her at home any longer and managed to get her into one of the homes of the National Society for Mentally Handicapped Children in Norfolk. This is a purpose-built home, catering for twenty severely sub-normal and terminal cases. She is very happy there and will be able to stay for the rest of her life. The story of how we finally got a diagnosis made would provide enough material for a book in itself but suffice to say that I got *no help whatsoever* from any of the various doctors, social workers and educationalists, etc. with whom I came into contact in my quest to find a cure for K, until I came across the Wolfson Centre. More of this later.

Since I last saw you K has attended three Rudolph Steiner schools. She had to leave them all because she was unmanageable and none of them gave any advice on where to send her next or on what her treatment should be. One day last October I came across a small article in a newspaper about a diagnostic unit in London called the Wolfson Centre, I showed it to my doctor who made an appointment for me to take K there. I really cannot describe adequately the feeling of relief and security that I experienced the moment we arrived at the Centre. There was no clinical atmosphere, no waiting in rows to be seen, no rush—not a white coat or stethoscope in sight— just a calm homely feeling everywhere. The doctor in charge of K's case took us to her office and assured us that even if it took years a diagnosis would be made, and that every support would be given to us by the Wolfson Centre when we decided where to send K.

Well it took four months of tests (K was an in-patient at Great Ormond Street at this time) to get a result, but the promised diagnosis was made. After that, the PSW of the Centre moved heaven and earth to get my local Authority to agree to pay K's fees to Hales House, which they did, and that is the current situation.

What still makes me so angry is, firstly that *nobody* ever told us about the Wolfson Centre even though it is well-known in medical and educational circles, and secondly that without the support of the centre, my Local Authority would not have agreed to send a terminal case to a Home. We had, at one point, a visit from a psychiatrist sent by our Authority putting very great pressure on us to put K in a mental hospital because, as he put it, 'if K is so subnormal she will not know if she is in good or bad surroundings'(!!). We visited —, which is supposed to be one of the best in the country and found the conditions there ghastly. There are forty beds to a ward about nine inches apart and all the children are sedated at night in order that the staff can cope. The staff are simply wonderful considering the appalling conditions they have to work with.

Do write your book and give encouragement to people not to give up and not to be pushed around by ignorant bureaucrats. We parents of handicapped children can help to get conditions improved if we dig in and insist on getting the best possible treatment instead of tamely agreeing that 'they' know best. The parent always knows best, as you have proved with Freddy. Do please mention the Wolfson Centre, Mecklenburgh Square, London, WC1. After my experience there, I'm sure that this place should be engraved on the minds of anyone who suspects that their child is abnormal in any way. Best of luck . . .

And from Yorkshire:

. . . T is now ten and still at his school for the deaf, and is still considered to be profoundly deaf plus speech difficulties. He has a very good teacher who is particularly interested in him—he is in a class of five children. We are waiting to see how the September report will turn out, as he will then have had one year with this teacher. He has progressed in reading and number work but speech and lip-reading are really just becoming meaningful and of use to him. He knows that screeching is objectionable and does not do it when we are out, but at home he likes to be objectionable some of the time, particularly when his older brother is around. He is very happy at school and in the school swimming team.

Happy New Year to you all.

And from the Midlands (Michael was now 13):

. . . In February last year, I requested that Michael be removed from the open-air school he was attending as there was only one teacher trained for children suffering from his difficulties and the others were both harsh and punitive with disastrous effects on Michael and no progress was made. The Local Authority agreed to him being transferred to another open air school. The teacher in charge of his class there had had no experience and although anxious to help, no progress was made. Michael then suffered an accident at football and was off school for three months. During this time an untrained student was found and Michael thrived on the one-to-one relationship and some slight progress was made. In September, a really good teacher appeared at the school. Remedially trained and experienced. Michael has made some progress BUT, this month, an appointment to see an educational psychologist a year ago, and cancelled on three occasions for different reasons, became a reality and a trip to London was made. This man spent the whole day on Michael and his verdict was that although eleven years old, Michael's reading age is that of a child of seven years five months. He said his intelligence is average but visual perception was often at the level of a four-year-old. He added that if he could have Michael in, to teach one hour daily, five days per week, for two years, he could see him achieving 'O' levels.

As we live miles apart, he suggested I advertise for someone who can apply special techniques and that it will cost 30/– per hour.

It is the Kinaesthetic approach which is required—learning through touch. This approach has been had at his open air school, but only for half-an-hour each week as only one member of the staff was trained to use it. Next term Michael will be eleven-and-a-half and will have to leave his school. There are four alternatives.

1. A Unit for delicate children at a bi-lateral school, in which most of the children suffer physical handicaps or are maladjusted.
2. The Remedial department of a comprehensive school where the children would be suffering all kinds of disorders and where the teachers are unlikely to have this necessary highly specialized training.
3. The local secondary modern school in the class for the backward, where again it will be most unlikely that the teachers are specially trained.
4. This is, that I get myself trained to do the Kinaesthetic approach and teach him myself after work. You will remember that I am a widow? I believe the equipment needed is expensive and I doubt if I shall be allowed to borrow from the Authority as I shall not have attended a proper official training . . .

195

I suggested she write to the Wolfson Centre to see if they knew of any special school concentrating on the Kinaesthetic approach. And from the mother of my god-son in South Āfrica came this:

. . . I don't know how long this thing of Paul being at the Rudolph Steiner is going to last. He went there too late in his life to adapt to it easily, and all the others are so *much* more handicapped than he is, that it makes him feel lonely and isolated. And yet, what alternative is there? Just to sit at home would be death to his spirit (and we'd go MAD) so we just press on, hoping. He so longs to have a JOB, but he needs protection, that is very clear. You must feel it too, but sometimes I feel so weighed *down* with care . . .

And from nearer home:

. . . David has lived all his thirteen years in M mostly in dreary vicarages in the poorer areas, but now, at last, in a fairly good environment (although without his father). His only talent so far is knitting! A total of sixty-six fluted tea-cosies, two rather splendid blankets and a number of baby blankets. I'm sick of it and it costs a fortune in wool . . .

A note on aphasia

The Shorter Oxford English Dictionary defines *aphasia* as 'Loss of the faculty of speech, as a result of cerebral affection.' The word was first used in 1864 by a French physician, Trousseau, to describe an acquired impairment of spoken language resulting from cerebral trauma or disease. The word *dysphasia* was subsequently introduced to mean a partial impairment of spoken language.

By analogy, neurologists applied the term *developmental aphasia* or *congenital aphasia* to the condition in which children fail to develop language normally apparently as a result of neurological impairment or dysfunction. It will be seen, however, that both by definition and clinically, the two conditions are not the same. This gave rise to confusion and some scepticism over the reality of developmental aphasia. Over the years, however, neurologists writing on the subject have described many cases of children of normal intelligence who failed to develop spoken language although deafness and severe personality disorder had been excluded. Developmental aphasia came to be defined, in fact, as 'the condition in which a child shows a relatively specific failure of the normal growth of language functions. The failure can manifest itself either in a disability in speaking with near normal speech understanding [*executive aphasia*] or in a disability in both understanding and expression of speech [*receptive aphasia*]. The disability is called a "specific" one because it cannot readily be ascribed to those factors which often provide the general setting in which failure of language development is usually observed, namely, deafness, mental deficiency, motor disability or severe personality disorder.' (Benton, A. L. (1964), 'Developmental aphasia and brain damage', *Cortex I,* 40-52.)

In a paper written in 1929 (Worster-Drought, C. and Allen,

I. M., 'Congenital auditory imperception', *J. Neur. Psychopath.*, 9, 139–208) it was suggested that the term *congenital auditory imperception* be applied to certain cases of developmental receptive aphasia for whom it might be a more meaningful description.

Aphasic children generally show a readiness to communicate in ways other than speech. Many display great ingenuity and skill in drawing and gesture. In this way they show evidence of symbolic function, simple concept development and social awareness, but their lack of adequate verbal language inevitably retards their cognitive and social development. Education, which depends so very heavily on language, presents, perhaps, the greatest problem of all.

Pauline Griffiths
Formerly Senior Speech Therapist, Invalid Children's Aid Association